BLUE GUIDE

ITALY
FOOD
COMPANION

Phrasebook & Miscellany

D0711279

Somerset Books • London

Blue Guide Italy Food Companion:
Phrasebook & Miscellany
First edition 2011

Published by Blue Guides Limited, a Somerset Books Company
Winchester House, Deane Gate Ave, Taunton, Somerset TA1 2UH
www.blueguides.com
'Blue Guide' is a registered trade mark.

© Blue Guides Limited 2011.
Compiled by Robin Saikia, Tonsor, Tom Brompton.

ISBN 978-1-905131-41-9

A CIP catalogue record of this book is available
from the British Library.

Distributed in the United States of America by WW Norton &
Company, Inc. of 500 Fifth Avenue, New York, NY 10110.

Illustrations by Jim Urquhart
Cover photo: © Geray Sweeney/CORBIS/Red Dot
Wine label by Anikó Kuzmich
Image pre-press by Hadley Kincade
Map by Dimap Bt.
Design and typesetting by Anikó Kuzmich, Blue Guides.

Printed and bound in Hungary by Pauker Nyomdaipari Kft.

CONTENTS

INTRODUCTION   4

HOW TO USE THIS BOOK   5

GLOSSARY & MISCELLANY   6

USEFUL PHRASES   185

I   The Twelve Basics   185
II   Finding a restaurant   185
III   Booking   187
IV   Basic questions   188
V   Arriving at the restaurant   189
VI   Ordering your meal   190
VII   Special needs and requests   194
VIII   When things go wrong   195
IX   Paying the bill   196
X   In the bar, café or gelateria   197

Map of Italy   199

INTRODUCTION

Italian food today is more popular than it has ever been and each year sees a new selection of very welcome books. More than half a century has passed since the publication in 1954 of Elizabeth David's classic, *Italian Food*, the book which showed English-speaking food-lovers that there was more to gastronomy than French cuisine and that much could be gained from an exploration of the diverse culinary heritage of the Italian peninsula. David's book was a great inspiration and many readers may remember the haphazard and tentative way in which we or our parents tried to recreate something of the Mezzogiorno in the cold northern reaches of post-war Britain. In the USA, meanwhile, a thriving Italian immigrant community had transplanted, preserved and developed the traditions of the old country. Over the last fifty years, both in Britain and North America, there has been a growing awareness of the vast regional diversity of Italy's food, vigorously promoted both by food writers and by Italian expatriate chefs. Excellent books have emerged, notably Gillian Riley's *Oxford Companion to Italian Food* and Oretta Zanini De Vita's *Encyclopedia of Pasta* (English translation by Maureen Fant). Both of these are essential reading for anyone interested in the subject of Italian food, as is *The Silver Spoon*, Phaidon's important English edition of the Italian classic first published in 1950.

This little miscellany in no way attempts to rival these books, either in scope or in scholarship. What it does offer is portability. This slim volume, sufficiently neat to put in a handbag or pocket, is designed to be a convenient tool for ready reference in restaurants, bars and cafés. We hope that readers will find it useful, entertaining and informative. Please do not hesitate to take us to task for any errors or omissions. The compilers are uneasily aware that there are rare, rich and obscure pastas made only on one day in the year in a secluded valley in Alto Adige, that have not made it into these pages. Please tell us about these and any other delights you may have experienced in the foothills of Monte Albo or on the shores of the wine-dark sea.

HOW TO USE THIS BOOK

The book is divided into two parts, a glossary and miscellany and a phrasebook. The Italian-English glossary contains short definitions of over 2,000 terms that one might expect to encounter, principally on menus. These range from simple translations of common food items to more obscure examples taken from local dialects and folklore. Some of the entries are longer and more discursive, such as those on pizza and truffles. Others have required little more than a line or word.

The English-Italian phrasebook begins with twelve essential words and phrases without which it is virtually impossible to make one's wishes, gastronomic or otherwise, known in Italy, among them 'Please', 'Thank you' and 'We would like'. These are followed by a series of practical phrases covering the essentials of dining: booking, ordering, asking advice, complaining, bestowing praise and, finally, paying the bill. Transliterations of all entries and phrases are given, in both glossary and phrasebook, so as to make them easy to pronounce. Comprehensive browsing of the glossary will, it is hoped, inspire readers to use the phrasebook in pursuit of ever more arcane delicacies. If a reader from Ascot or Alabama marches purposefully into a bar in a remote area of Molise demanding *ciufele* and Tintilia, this book will not have been written in vain.

GLOSSARY & MISCELLANY

abbacchio [a-**bah**-kee-oh] a milk-fed lamb no more than four weeks old, popular in Rome and elsewhere in Lazio, also known as *agnellino da latte*, 'little lamb of milk'. *Abbacchio* is cooked in variety of ways, often roasted or casseroled. *Abbacchio scottadito* are cutlets, preferably charcoal-grilled.

abboccato [ah-boh-**kah**-toh] semi-dry, very slightly sweet (wine).

abbotta pezziende [ah-**boh**-tah-pet-see-**end**-ay] 1. soft, sweet bread roll from Molise, flavoured with sugar and lemon; 2. a stew, typically with beans and chickpeas; 3. SEE SAGNE A PEZZE.

abbrustolito/a [ah-broosto-**lee**-toh] toasted, e.g. *pane abbrustolito*: toast.

abissini [ah-bi-**seen**-ee] the smallest type of shell-shaped pasta, suitable for soups. They were named after Italy's former African colony. Nowadays they are more commonly known as *cocciolette*. They resemble small CONCHIGLIE.

Abruzzo [ah-**broots**-oh] mountainous region in the centre of the Italian peninsula known for its durum wheat, used for a wide variety of pastas, which are often flavoured with PEPERONCINO, another local speciality. Other noted Abruzzese products are nougat (*torrone*) and lentils. Montepulciano d'Abruzzo is the best-known wine.

acciuga [atch-**oo**-gah] (pl. *acciughe*) anchovy, preserved in salt, which turns them a distinctive silvery-brown colour. Salted whole, their flavour is enhanced by the gradual disintegration of their bones and intestines—perhaps a modern-day survival of the popular ancient Roman fish sauce called garum, which was made from salted and fermented fish guts. Fresh anchovies are known as ALICI.

acerbo [atch-**air**-boh] sour, unripe or harsh.

aceto [atch-**ay**-toh] vinegar.

aceto balsamico [atch-**ay**-toh bal-**sammy**-coe] traditional balsamic vinegar is produced in and around Modena in Emilia-Romagna and is made mainly using the local white grape, Trebbiano di Castelvetro. It is misleadingly named, since it is not a vinegar but a syrup made from grape must, subjected to a lengthy and sophisticated ageing process. The must is boiled down to a sweet syrup which is left to ferment for a year or more in a barrel. After this initial period of fermentation, the must is decanted each year into a series of progressively smaller barrels (as time goes on, moisture evaporates) made from a variety of different woods, each of which, connoisseurs insist, impart different flavours. Standard balsamic vinegar (not *Tradizionale*) is made with a mixture of reduced must (*mosto cotto*) and wine vinegar. As with wine, there is a bewildering spectrum of quality and price. There are even *Riserva* vinegars. The age of the finished product— some vinegars have been aged for almost a century--makes a spectacular difference to taste and price.

acetosella [ah-chet-oh-**zell**-ah] sorrel.

acido [atch-**ee**-doh] sour, acidic, sharp-tasting.

acidulo [atch-**ee**-doo-low] high in acid (but not necessarily unpleasant), tart.

acini di pepe [atch-**ee**-nee dee **pay**-pay] tiny, pellet-shaped pasta mainly used in soups.

acino [atch-**ee**-no] grape.

acqua minerale [**ack**-wah me-nay-**rah**-lay] mineral water. *Acqua gassata* or *acqua frizzante* is fizzy water. *Acqua liscia* or *senza gas* is still water. Useful phrases to know when ordering water are *con/senza ghiaccio* (with/without ice [**gyah**-choh]) and *temperatura ambiente* (room temperature).

acqua pazza [**ack**-wah **pat**-zah] literally 'mad water', referring to a recipe for poached white fish, which in the Naples area were cooked in seawater seasoned with herbs, tomatoes and wine. The 'mad water' is the broth itself. The phrase is said to originate in Tuscany, where peasants would boil the seeds, stems, grapeskins and pulp left over from wine production and leave the mush to ferment for several days. The resulting 'mad water' was a much less pleasant drink than wine but often just as intoxicating and a great deal cheaper to produce.

acquadella [ack-wah-**day**-lah] see LATTERINO.

Acqualagna see TRUFFLES.

acquasale [ack-wah-**sah**-lay] literally 'dirty water', a thin soup from Basilicata made by pouring a broth made of onions, tomatoes and garlic over slices of dried or stale bread.

acquaviti [ack-wah-**vee**-tee] liqueurs made from distilled grapes or fruit, like German *Schnaps*.

affettati [ah-fay-**tah**-tee] cold cuts, sliced meats.

affogato/a [ah-fo-**gah**-toh] poached.

affogato al caffè [ah-fo-**gah**-toh al ka-**feh**] ice cream doused with hot ESPRESSO.

affumicato/a [a-foom-ee-**kah**-toh] smoked.

aframomo [afra-**moh**-moh] Melegueta pepper, grains of paradise, a peppery spice from the ginger family, native to West Africa (*Aframomum melegueta*).

agghiotta di pesce spada [aggy-**oh**-tah dee **pay**-shay **spa**-dah] a popular Sicilian recipe for swordfish (*pesce* = fish, *spada* = sword), made with garlic, from the Sicilian *agghia*, a variant of the standard Italian word for garlic, *aglio*.

Aglianico [ah-**lyan**-ee-koh] hardy red-wine grape from Campania and Basilicata widely celebrated as the 'noblest' grape of the south. It was the grape used in the ancient Falernian wine, praised by Pliny. Today it is the main grape in Taurasi.

agliata [ah-**lyah**-tah] a kind of garlic mayonnaise made from garlic, egg yolk and olive oil whipped together until creamy (Liguria).

aglio [ah-lee-oh] garlic; two Italian strains with protected geographical status (DOP) are Aglio Bianco Polesano from the Veneto and Aglio di Voghiera from Emilia-Romagna.

aglio e olio [**ah**-lee-oh ay **oh**-le-oh] also known as *olio e aglio*, 'garlic and olive oil', a quick sauce for pasta, often with PEPERONCINO and parsley.

aglio orsino [**ah**-lee-oh or-**see**-no] wild garlic.

agnello [an-**yell**-oh] lamb, a weaned lamb, therefore older than an ABBACCHIO and having a stronger flavour. It is usually roasted or stewed and served *alla pastora* (with potatoes) or *cacio e uova* (stuffed with

grated PECORINO cheese and eggs, a method widespread in Abruzzo and Molise, where it is known as *agnill cac'e 'ove*.

agnolini [ann-yo-**lee**-nee] *see agnolotti*.

agnolotti [ann-yo-**loh**-tee] sometimes known as *agnolini*, a Piedmontese PASTA RIPIENA, in effect a type of RAVIOLI. Originally they were a way of using leftover roast meat, which is why the traditional filling is a meat sauce. They are sometimes served in broth and can also be covered in melted butter and sage.

agone [a-**go**-nay] the lake shad, a fish found in Lake Como (pl. *agoni*).

agresto [a-**grays**-toh] a tart-tasting condiment, known as verjuice in English; a concentrate obtained from the juice of unripened grapes and used to impart a sour tang to sauces.

agretti [a-**grett**-ee] also known as *barba di frate* ('friar's beard'); saltwort. The leaves are either used as a salad vegetable, eaten pickled or very lightly braised. The taste is slightly salty, faintly reminiscent of fresh spinach.

agric. biol. frequently used on menus, the abbreviation for *agricoltura biologica*: organic farming.

agro [**ah**-groh] sour; *all' agro*, with olive oil and lemon juice.

agrodolce [**ah**-groh **doll**-chay] sweet and sour. Recipes vary regionally and according to the meat or vegetables for which the *salsa agrodolce* is destined.

agrumi [ah-**groo**-mee] citrus fruits.

aguglia [ah-**gool**-ee-ah] the garfish, a long, needle-shaped seawater fish (pl. *aguglie*).

al, all' alla in the style of, e.g. *alla rustica*: country style; *al forno*: in the oven, baked.

ala [**ah**-lah] wing, e.g. *ala di pollo*: chicken wing.

alaccia [ah-**latch**-ah] shad, a bony fish of the herring family.

alalonga [ah-la-**long**-ah] long-

fin tuna.

Alba [**ahl**-bah] town in Piedmont that hosts an annual truffle fair in autumn (see TARTUFO) and which is also known for its BARBERA wine.

Alba madonna [**ahl**-bah mah-**doan**-ah] a white truffle (see TARTUFO).

albicocca [al-bee-**cock**-ah] apricot (pl. *albicocche*).

Alchermes [al-**kair**-mays] a scarlet, slightly bitter-tasting liqueur made from flowers and spices, traditionally used in the making of ZUPPA INGLESE.

Aleatico [ah-lay-**ah**-tee-koh] red-wine grape that grows throughout central Italy (Tuscany, Lazio, Umbria, Marche) and also in Puglia, where it is the principal ingredient of the fruity red wines of the Salento peninsula, the heel of Italy. It is also used to make a sweet dessert wine, described by Napoleon as one of the few available consolations during his exile on the island of Elba.

alfabeto [al-fah-**bay**-toh] internationally popular PASTINA representing the letters of the alphabet.

alfredo [al-**fray**-doh] a cream, butter and cheese sauce, named after Alfredo di Lelio, whose restaurant in Rome, Alfredo alla Scrofa, was patronised by Mary Pickford and Douglas Fairbanks in the 1920s. They were captivated by di Lelio's FETTUCCINE and presented him with a gold knife and fork in recognition of his services to gastronomy. The restaurant still exists, as does its successor establishment, Il Vero Alfredo, just a few blocks away from the original, on Piazza Augusto Imperatore.

alici [ah-**lee**-chee] anchovies, served freshly caught or halved and preserved in brine rather than the salted kind (ACCIUGA).

alisanzas [ah-lee-**zant**-sas] also *sas alisanzas* [**sass** ah-lee-**zant**-sass], a Sardinian long pasta typically served with a robust meat RAGÙ.

allevamento, all' [a-lay-vah-**mayn**-toh] farmed, farm-reared (of fish and game), i.e. not wild. An *allevatore* is a farmer, breeder.

allodola [a-**load**-oh-lah] the lark, a small game bird, roasted whole and served *in spiedini* (on skewers) or served in pies; pl. *allodole*.

alloro, foglia di [**foe**-lee-ah dee a-**lor**-oh] bay leaf.

alosa [a-**low**-zah] shad, a freshwater relative of the herring, also known as *cheppia*.

alpestre see ARQUEBUSE.

alta cucina [al-tah koo-**chee**-nah] *haute cuisine*.

Alto Adige see TRENTINO.

amabile [a-**mah**-bee-lay] of wine, slightly sweet.

amandola [a-**man**-doe-lah] almond (pl. *amandole*).

amarena [a-mah-**ray**-nah] the bitter Morello cherry, often preserved in syrup or brandy.

amaretti [a-mah-**ret**-ee] traditional almond biscuits, hard and crunchy.

Amaretto [a-mah-**ret**-oh] almond-based liqueur.

amaro/a [ah-**mah**-roh] adj.
bitter. Amaro is also the name
of a bitter DIGESTIVO flavoured
with herbs.

Amaro Averna [ah-**mah**-roh
ah-**vair**-nah] a caramelised
herbal DIGESTIVO from Sicily,
very popular throughout Italy.

Amarone [ah-mah-**roan**-ay]
full-bodied, highly-regarded
(and invariably expensive)
VALPOLICELLA wine (dry red)
made from selected bunches
of Corvina grapes that are
dried (raisined) before press-
ing. The wine is aged for at
least five years and is notably high in alcohol content.
Compare RECIOTO.

amatriciana [ah-mah-tree-
chah-nah] a popular pasta
sauce of tomatoes, PECORINO
cheese, PANCETTA and chilli,
a Roman recipe originating
from Amatrice in northern
Lazio. In origin, the sauce
does not contain tomatoes;
they came to dominate the
mixture after their arrival
from the New World.

ambrato [am-**brah**-toh]
white wine that has turned a
darker shade, slightly amber,
through oxidation.

Americano [ah-may-ree-**kah**-
noh] 1. a cocktail consisting of equal measures of
red vermouth and CAMPARI
topped up with soda water;
2. *caffè americano* or *caffè
all'americana* is filter coffee or
percolated coffee. The effect
can also be achieved by adding water to *espresso*.

ammazzacaffè [ah-**mats**-ah-
kah-**fay**] lit. 'coffee-killer', a
small shot of liqueur drunk
after a coffee. A chaser.

ammogghiu [a-**mog**-ee-you]
a rich Sicilian dressing of
ripe tomatoes, RICOTTA, basil,
chilli, garlic, salt and olive oil.

analcolico [ann-al-**kohl**-ee-
ko] non-alcoholic. *Bevande
analcoliche* = alcohol-free
drinks.

ananas [**ahn**-an-ass] pine-
apple.

anatra [**ahn**-at-rah] sometimes called *anitra* [**ahn**-eat-
rah] duck, often stuffed. In
Venetian dialect the *anatra*

ripiena (stuffed duck) is often referred to as *anara col pien*. The stuffing is made of duck liver, breadcrumbs, raisins, egg, cheese, herbs and crumbled AMARETTI biscuits. The wild duck of the Venetian lagoon is celebrated in Carpaccio's painting of Venetian sportsmen (Getty Museum, Los Angeles) where several ducks can be seen scudding across the sky.

anchellini [ann-kell-**ee**-nee] 'little anchors', also known as *piombi* (weights), pasta served in soups.

anelli, anelletti, anellini [ann-**ell**-ee, ann-ell-**ett**-ee, ann-ell-**ee**-nee] 'little rings', a pasta shape said to be based on the earrings worn by the women of Benghazi, one of Italy's former colonies; *anelli Siciliani*, 'Sicilian rings', are the larger type.

aneto [ann-**ay**-toh] dill.

angelica [ann-**jay**-lee-kah] wild parsnip; the seeds and roots are used to flavour GRAPPA; the stems are put to a variety of uses, candied as sweetmeats or thinly sliced and tossed with slices of Parma ham; leaves are eaten raw in salads.

anguilla [an-**gwee**-lah] eel, served in a variety of regional styles, usually stewed. Some of the best freshwater eels are said to come from Lake Bolsena in Lazio. Another important source is the Comacchio lagoon in Emilia-Romagna.

anguria [ann-**goo**-ree-ah] watermelon.

anice [ann-**ee**-chay] anise, a small plant of the parsley family with a distinctive liquorice flavour.

animelle [anny-**mell**-ay] sweetbreads, the thymus glands of a young calf, usually breaded, sautéed, grilled or chopped and used in pastas as a filling; known as *lacetti* in Piedmont. In Lazio, *animelle* are often taken to refer either to the thymus gland or the pancreas of a calf or sheep.

Anisetta [ah-nee-**zet**-ah] anise-flavoured liqueur from the Marche.

annegati [ann-ay-**gah**-tee] slices of meat marinated in white wine or MARSALA sauce.

annoso [ah-**noh**-zoh] of wine, aged.

anolini [ah-no-**lee**-nee] PASTA RIPIENA from Emilia-Romagna, typically stuffed with beef that has been stewed until it falls apart its own juices. The pasta itself is usually cooked in broth.

antipasti [ann-tee-**pas**-tee] starters, *hors d'oeuvres*; literally 'before a meal'. These often consist of a selection of cured meat or fish.

antipastino [ann-tee-pas-**tee**-no] a little appetiser, something more than a *bonne bouche* (ASSAGGIO) and less than a full-blown *antipasto*.

antiveleno [ann-tee-vay-**lay**-no] antidote, the 'hair of the dog'.

aperitivi [a-pair-ee-**tee**-vee] drinks taken before a meal to stimulate appetite; aperitifs.

Aperol Spritz [**ah**-pair-ol **spreets**] a popular Venetian *aperitivo* made with PROSECCO and Aperol orange liqueur, topped up with soda water.

aperto [ah-**pair**-toh] open.

apiciano [ah-pee-**chah**-noh] 'Apician' (pl. *apiciani*). A dish or dishes described thus on a menu is making reference to the Roman gourmet Apicius (*see box opposite*).

arachidi [a-**rack**-ee-dee] peanuts.

aragosta [ah-rah-**ghost**-ah] the rock lobster (*see illustration on p. 19*), a clawless species of crawfish or langouste (*Palinurus elephas*).

arancia [ah-**ran**-chah] orange; a winter fruit, grown in southern Italy, in season from November to February. A *sanguinello* is a 'blood orange', as is a *moro* and a *tarocco*. The *tarocco*, a sweet, seedless variety native to Italy, reputedly derives its name from the expression of wonder, satisfaction and greed uttered by the peasant who first saw one: 'Tarocco!' he exclaimed, as one might when winning a trick in the card game *Tarocchi* or one of its variants: 'We've come up trumps with this one!'

aranciata [ah-ran-**chah**-tah] orangeade, orange soda, a fizzy drink, as opposed to *spremuta di arancia* (freshly squeezed orange juice).

arancini [ah-ran-**chee**-nee] fried or baked rice balls, coated with breadcrumbs, typical of Sicily, where they are said to have been introduced by the Arabs. The breadcrumb outer crust turns golden-or-ange when cooked, hence the name. The standard filling is a RAGÙ of meat, peas, rice and MOZZARELLA, but many other fillings are found (mushroom, sausage, PROSCIUTTO). Arancini are usually round, but they can also be cone-shaped. In Roman cuisine, SUPPLÌ are similar to *arancini*. In Naples, rice balls are called *palline di riso*.

Apicius

Marcus Gavius Apicius (AD 14–37) was a famous epicure whose name is pseudoepigraphically linked to a book of ancient Roman recipes. It is unlikely that Apicius wrote these recipes down, though he would certainly have eaten many of them: he has gained a reputation for lavishness and extravagance that is not entirely fair. It is true that gourmet recipes do form a chapter in the book, but the main accent is on the method of preparation and the importance of condiments. The version of *agrodolce* (sweet and sour) sauce mentioned in Apicius, for example, recommends the use of 'pepper, mint, pine nuts, sultanas, carrots, honey, vinegar, oil, wine and musk'.

Arbëreshe [arh-buh-**ray**-shay] the Albanian communi-ty of southern Italy and Sicily, who retain a distinct cuisine.

arborio [ar-**bor**-ee-oh] a type of glutinous, short-grain rice from the Po valley, typically used in RISOTTO.

ardente [arr-**dayn**-tay] literally 'burning', high in alcohol content (wine).

aringa [arr-**eeng**-ah] herring, also *renga* (pl. *renge*).

arista [arr-**east**-ah] in Florence, a lean cut of pork.

arlecchino [ar-leck-**ee**-noh] a 'harlequin', a colourful selection or mixture, often of vegetables, e.g. *arlecchino di verdure al vapore*: a mixture of steamed vegetables.

armelin [ar-may-**leen**] in the dialect of northeastern Italy, an apricot.

armonie [ar-**moan**-ee-ay] also known as *stortini*, a pasta served in soups.

Arneis [ar-**nay**-ees] a white grape from Piedmont used to produce dry, flowery wines.

arnia [**ar**-nee-ah] a beehive.

aromi, aromati [ah-**roam**-ee, a-roam-**ah**-tee] a general term for aromatic herbs like rosemary, thyme, basil, oregano.

arquebuse [ark-way-**boo**-zay] a herbal DIGESTIVO from Piedmont. Also known as *alpestre*. See TANACETO.

arrabbiata [ah-rah-bee-**ah**-tah] popular pasta sauce made of garlic, tomato and chilli. The name literally translates as 'enraged'.

arraganato/a [ah-rah-gah-**nah**-toh] a dish thus described is covered with herbs and breadcrumbs, and oven-baked.

arrosticini [ah-rost-ee-**chee**-nee] skewered pieces of meat, often lamb, popular in Abruzzo and Molise; kebabs.

arrosto [ah-**rost**-oh] as a noun, a roast; as an adjective, roasted. *Pollo arrosto* = roast chicken.

arselle [ar-**sell**-ay] tiny clams, also known as TELLINE or *zighe*. They are often served in broth with FREGULA. *Arselle* is sometimes incorrectly used to denote scallops, the correct names for which are either *pettini, cappasante* or CAPESANTE.

Artusi, Pellegrino (1820–1911)
A silk merchant from Forlì in Emilia-Romagna who wrote a best-selling cookbook, *La scienza in cucina e l'arte di mangiare bene* (*The Science of Cooking and the Art of Eating Well*). Having made a fortune in silk, Artusi devoted himself to his favourite pastimes, eating and collecting recipes. Unable to find a publisher for the resulting collection of notes and anecdotes, he published the work himself in 1891, at the age of 71. By the time of his death it had sold over 200,000 copies and remains in print in several languages to this day. The most extensive edition is edited by the historian Piero Camporesi. The book is important because it was the first major work on Italian food to appear since the unification of Italy in 1861. It was Artusi who identified turpentine as the best means of neutralising the smell of urine after eating asparagus. A few drops in a chamber pot, or these days in the lavatory pan, convert the strange aroma of asparagus into a flowery fragrance.

asiago [ah-zee-**ah**-goh] cow's milk cheese from the Veneto and Trentino, available as *asiago d'allevo* (the artisanal variety) or *asiago pressato* (processed, and much milder in taste).

asino [ah-**zee**-noh] donkey, donkey meat, steadily attaining status as a rarity and therefore a delicacy; *stracotto d'asino*, donkey stew, is made with red wine and juniper berries and plenty of butter and lard. It is typically served with POLENTA.

asparagi [as-**parra**-jee] asparagus. Both white and green varieties are available across Italy. Young spears are boiled, steamed or roasted and dressed with olive oil

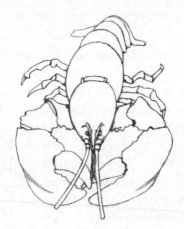

Above: *astice*, true lobster, with pincers. Below right: *aragosta*, the clawless lobster or rock lobster.

and grated cheese; *asparagi selvatici* or *di campo* = wild asparagus.

aspretto [as-**pret**-oh] pleasantly sharp (wine).

asprigno/a [as-**preen**-yoh] pleasantly tart.

aspro/a [as-**proh**] sour, bitter.

assabesi [ass-ah-**bay**-zee] shortbread biscuits flavoured with hazelnuts and cocoa powder named in honour of Italy's purchase of the port of Assab in Eritrea in 1869. There was a fashion at the time for naming food items after Italy's colonies.

assaggio [ah-**sadge**-oh] a taster, from *assaggiare*, to try, to sample. ASSAGGI [a-**sadge**-ee] are a selection of little tasters or small portions.

Associazione Verace Pizza Napoletana the Authentic Neapolitan Pizza Association, a body dedicated to preserving the integrity of local pizza, ensuring that makers who use the best local ingredients, such as DOP San Marzano tomatoes and DOP MOZZARELLA cheese, are granted due recognition.

assortimento [ah-sorty-**main**-toh] an assortment.

Asti Spumante [**ass**-tee spoo-**mahn**-tee] a sweet to medium-sweet sparkling wine from Asti in Piedmont. Despite a harsh press from wine snobs, Asti Spumante has a respectable pedigree. It was invented by the Duke of Savoy's jeweller, Giovanni Battista Croce, around the beginning of the 17th century. When Croce retired he embarked on a successful second career as a viticulturalist, producing a varied and popular range of wines using the MOSCATO grape.

astice [as-**tee**-chay] lobster (*see illustration opposite*).

attesa [ah-**tay**-zah] waiting time, e.g. *attesa: 15 minuti*, sometimes found on menus beside dishes which require special preparation.

aumm aumm [owm-owm] aubergine and MOZZARELLA sauce from Capri, usually eaten with PENNE.

avemarie [**ah**-vay-mah-**ree**-ay] small pasta shapes that cook quickly, ready in just the time it takes to recite a Hail Mary. See PATERNOSTER.

avena [ah-**vay**-nah] oat.

Averna see AMARO.

azarole [at-sah-**role**-ay] an orange-red, bittersweet, vitamin-rich fruit of the hawthorn family.

azzimo [**ad**-zee-moh] unleavened.

azzurro [ad-**zoo**-roh] blue,

as in the generic description *pesce azzurro*, 'blue fish', stronger tasting, darker-fleshed fish such as *tonno* (tuna), *sgombro* (mackerel), *aringa* (herring), *pesce spada* (swordfish) and *acciuga* (anchovy).

babà [bah-**bah**] a Neapolitan rum-soaked pastry of French origin, shaped like a fat mushroom. It was allegedly invented to console Stanislaw Leszczinsky after his defeat in the War of the Polish Succession in 1735.

bacan [bah-**can**] in the Veneto, a farmer; seen on menus as

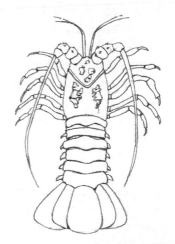

suggestive of authenticity.

bàcaro [**bah**-kah-roh] a typical Venetian wine shop or wine bar serving drinks, snacks and simple meals. You would typically go to a *bàcaro* in the early evening for an OMBRA and CICCHETI.

bacca [**bah**-ka] berry (pl. *bacche*).

baccalà [back-ah-**lah**] salt cod, served in a variety of ways, usually de-salted by soaking in water, cut into portions and fried, served with regional sauce and pasta. *Baccalà alla vicentina*, a Vicenza dish, uses unsalted cod; *baccalà alla romana* is a speciality of Roman Jewish cuisine. Menus will sometimes offer a more generic *baccalà fritto*, a simple cod-in-batter starter that echoes the best of British fish and chips. *Baccalà mantecato*, in Venetian dialect *bacaeà mantecà*, consists of boiled STOCCAFISSO beaten with olive oil and seasoning into a thick pâté and served spread over bread or POLENTA.

baccarella [back-ah-**rell**-ah] in Corsica, an immense tuna, the stuff of tall tales.

bacio [**batch**-oh] literally, 'a kiss'; in confectionery, *baci* are chocolate and hazelnut sweets, made in Perugia, Umbria.

bagna cauda [**ban**-ya **cow**-da] literally, a 'hot bath', a hot dip made with anchovies, olive oil and garlic, accompanying a selection of raw or cooked vegetables. See also BAGNÈT and BAGNUN.

bagnèt [ban-**yet**] in Piedmont dialect, a 'little bath', a sauce for *bollito misto*, a selection of boiled meats. There are two species of *bagnèt*, red and green. *Bagnèt ross*, or *bagnetto rosso*, is made with tomatoes, carrots, onions and garlic, simmered in wine vinegar with a teaspoonful of sugar. *Bagnèt verd*, or *bagnetto verde*, is made with anchovies, parsley, garlic, vinegar, bread and olive oil.

bagnun [ban-**yoon**] literally a 'big bath' or 'big dip', a Ligurian soup made with fresh anchovies, onion, olive oil, bread and tomatoes. It is easy to make and was therefore popular with fishermen. Today it is something of a cult dish. It even has its own website (www.bagnun.it).

balacin [bah-lah-**cheen**] see FRICO BALACIA.

balilla [bah-**lee**-lah] a soft rice with a melting texture, often used for desserts and ARANCINI.

ballerine [bah-lay-**ree**-nay] pasta shapes, literally 'ballerinas', because they resemble a pretty dress; also known as *campanelle*, 'little bells'.

balsamico see ACETO BALSAMICO.

banchetto [ban-**ket**-oh] banquet.

barattolo [bah-**rah**-toh-loh] a can, *un barattolo di birra* is a can of beer; *dodici barattoli di birra* is 12 cans of beer.

barbabietola [bar-bah-bee-**ay**-toh-lah] beetroot.

barbaforte [bar-bah-**four**-tay] horseradish.

barbagiuai [bar-bah-jee-**why**] a type of fried RAVIOLI from Liguria filled with a mixture of pumpkin and cheese. *Barbagiuai* means, in local dialect 'Uncle Giovanni' (*barba* = uncle; lit. 'bearded one'; *giuai* = Giovanni). A certain Giovanni allegedly invented the dish.

Barbaresco [bar bah-**ray**-skoh] highly-regarded red wine from Piedmont, like BAROLO made from the NEBBIOLO grape (the two wine regions are near neighbours). Typically tannins are softer in a Barbaresco, making the wine quicker to mature than Barolo. Angelo Gaja is one of the most famous producers.

Barbera [bar-**bey**-ra] red grape of Piedmont and Lombardy, used to make increasingly fine wine, fruity and dark in colour. A *Barbera Superiore* is an aged Barbera, a *Barbera Barricato* has been aged in a *barrique*, a French-style wooden cask.

barbina [bar-**bee**-nah] 'little beard', strand-shaped pasta.

barbozzo [bar-**bot**-zoh] cured pig's cheek, an Umbrian speciality.

bardele con morai [bar-**day**-lay con moh-**rye**] a pasta from the Veneto and Lombardy, served with butter, PARMESAN and sage leaves.

Bardolino [bar-doh-**lee**-noh] a popular light red wine from the province of Verona. There is a rosé version, the *Bardolino Chiaretto*, and a *Bardolino Novello*, the new growth released annually in the same manner as Beaujolais Nouveau. The *Bardolino Superiore* has an extra 1 percent strength.

Barolo [ba-**roh**-low] one of the great Italian red wines, rich, full-flavoured and high in tannin. It is made from the NEBBIOLO grape, grown around the village of Barolo in the low hills of Piedmont.

basilico [bah-**zee**-lee-koh] basil. Often used in tomato sauces, pizza, salads, soups and omelettes, it is also the basis for PESTO. Basil has powerful symbolic connotations of fertility and kingship—the name derives from the Greek *basileus* meaning king—and is believed to have flourished on the site in the Holy Land where St Helen discovered the True Cross.

bastardui [bas-tar-**doo**-ee] pasta from Liguria served in a creamy leek sauce.

bastunaca [bas-toon-**ack**-ah] in Calabria and Sicily, the wild carrot.

batata [bat-**aht**-ah] yam, sweet potato.

batsoà [bat-so-**ah**] in Piedmont, meat from a pig's foot, marinated in vinegar, dipped in batter and fried.

battolli [bat-**oll**-ee] pasta from Liguria, made with chestnut flour and often served with PESTO ALLA GENOVESE.

battuta [bah-**too**-tah] literally 'pounded', 'beaten'. *Battuta di manzo* is steak tartare. *Battuta di pollo* is a kind of chicken terrine.

battuto [bah-**too**-toh] a mixture of chopped vegetables such as onion, garlic, celery and carrot mixed with herbs and fat (oil, butter or lard) and used to flavour a stew or soup—in other words, a freshly-made stock cube. *Battuta* means beaten or pulverised, in this case with a pestle and mortar. When sautéed, the same ingredients would constitute a SOFFRITTO.

bavarese [bah-vah-**ray**-zay] a rich cake of Bavarian origin made with ice cream and whipped cream, made popular by German visitors to northern Italy.

bavette [bah-**vet**-eh] literally, 'strings of drool', a popular if unappetisingly nicknamed pasta. *Bavette* are served with a variety of regional sauces, notably tuna and capers in the Sicilian archipelago.

bazzotto [bad-**zot**-oh] coddled (of an egg).

beccaccia [beck-**atch**-ah] woodcock.

beccaccino [beck-atch-**een**-oh] snipe.

beccafico [beck-ah-**fee**-koh] lit. 'figpecker', a small songbird, a warbler. Of the more *recherché* Ligurian recipes *beccafichi nel nido* [**nee**-doh], 'warblers in their nests', stands out. The warblers are seasoned and then roasted on a 'nest' consisting of a large mushroom cap.

beciamella, besciamella [betcha-**mell**-ah, besh-ah-**mell**-ah] Italian transliteration of béchamel, the white sauce made from butter and milk, thickened with flour.

belecot [bel eh-**kot**] spiced minced pork (Emilia-Romagna).

Bellini [bell-**ee**-nee] a cocktail of fresh peach juice and PROSECCO, invented at Harry's Bar in Venice. As the CARPACCIO is named after one Venetian artist, so is this after another.

Bel Paese [bell pie-**ay**-zay] a mild, industrially-produced cheese (made of cow's milk), originating in Melzo in Lombardy, named after a bestselling 19th-century work of popular science by the geologist-priest Father Antonio Stoppani. The book, *Il Bel Paese* (*The Beautiful Country*) consists of 32 fireside 'conversations' extolling the beauties of the Italian landscape and explaining concepts of natural science in straightforward, comprehensible language.

berlingozzo [bear-lean-**got**-soh] a sweet bread (Florence).

bernese [bear-**nay**-zay] béarnaise sauce, made of clarified butter and emulsified egg yolks with herbs and seasoning.

bertagnin [bear-tan-**yeen**] salt cod, *baccalà* (Venice).

bertù [bear-**too**] stuffed pasta from Lombardy, filled with sausage, PARMESAN and egg.

bevanda [bay-**van**-dah] a drink, beverage (pl. *bevande*).

bianchetto [bee-ann-**ket**-oh] whitebait or herring (pl. *bianchetti*).

bianco [bee-**ann**-koh] 1. white (wine); 2. *in bianco*: cooked without tomatoes; the opposite of *in rosso*. Recipes that require a sauce *in bianco* often predate the arrival of tomatoes from the New World.

bianco carta [bee-**ann**-koh **car**-tah] a clear, almost colourless white wine.

biancomangiare [bee-**ann**-koh-man-**jar**-ay] a dish dating back to the Middle Ages, often translated as 'blancmange', though the original Italian version could be sweet or savoury. The guiding principal of preparation was the whiteness of the ingredients, which could include cheese, chicken, rice or fish. At its heart, however, a *biancomangiare* was an almond pudding, and it is as a sweet dessert that it mainly survives today, prepared with ground almonds soaked either in cow's milk or almond milk and thickened with cornflour or set with gelatin.

biavetta [bee-ah-**vet**-ah] a tiny, rice-shaped egg pasta from Piedmont, the basis of *minestra del bate 'l gran*, 'bash-the-wheat' soup, a hearty chicken broth served to harvest workers at threshing time.

bibita [bib-**eet**-ah] a soft drink, pl. *bibite* [bib-**ee**-tay].

bicchiere [bicky-**ay**-ray] a drinking glass. Wine prices are quoted by the *bicchiere* or by the *bottiglia*.

bicchiere della staffa [bicky-**ay**-ray della **stah**-fah] one for the road, literally a *bicchiere* (glass) before I reach for my *staffa* (my wayfarer's staff).

bicchierino [bicky-ay-**ree**-noh] a paper cup for ice cream, or a small glass, usually for wine.

bicerin [bitch-air-**een**] coffee, hot chocolate and whipped cream, a Turin speciality.

bietola [bee-**ay**-toh-lah] Swiss chard, a species of beetroot bred for its leaves rather than its roots (pl. *bietole*).

bietolone [bee-ay-toh-**loan**-ay] an outsize Swiss chard.

biga [**bee**-gah] a substantial sourdough bread.

bigarade [bee-gah-**rah**-day] meat sauce made with orange juice and citrus zest.

bignè [been-**yay**] the Italian cream puff, related to the French *beignet*, also known as *bigné di San Giuseppe* because it is traditionally served on St Joseph's day, 19th March.

bigoli [**bee**-go-lee] a pasta (literally 'worms') from Friuli-Venezia Giulia, a robust spaghetti-like variety. The strands are thick and hollow, making it an ideal vehicle for sauces. *Bigoli col'anara* is a substantial Paduan dish in which the pasta is served in a sauce made of duck livers seasoned with sage. *Bigoli co le sardele* is a dish of *bigoli* pasta with a sauce of sardines. *Bigoli col tocio* are served in a minced meat RAGÙ.

bigui [**bee**-gwi] = BIGOLI.

biovette [bee-oh-**vet**-ay] soft, plump bread rolls (Piedmont).

biroldo [bee-**roll**-doe] a sausage from western Tuscany made of pork and pig's blood seasoned with garlic, lemon peel and parsley and incorporating raisins and pine nuts.

birra [bee-rah] beer; *birra chiara* [key-**ah**-rah] is light beer, lager; *birra rossa* [**ross**-ah] or *scura* [**skoo**-rah] is dark beer. In central and northern regions of Italy there may be an emphasis on German beers, but Italians are justifiably proud of native brews such as Nastro Azzurro, brewed by Peroni in Lombardy.

birreria [bee-ray-**ree**-yah] a beer bar.

bisatto [bee-**zah**-toh] a Venetian word for an eel.

biscotti [bees-**kot**-ee] a generic term for biscuits, in all their regional manifestations (and there are many). The word means cooked (*cotto*) twice (*bis*), descriptive of the preliminary part-baking of a solid lump of dough which is then sliced or cut into shapes before the second and final turn in the oven.

bistecca [bee-**steck**-ah] steak (*see box below*).

Steaks and how to order them

Bistecca di maiale is a pork chop. If what you want is beef, make sure you are ordering *bistecca di manzo* [**mant**-soh]. The famous *bistecca alla fiorentina* [fee-oh-rain-**teen**-ah] is a thick T-bone of CHIANINA beef. Purists eat it very rare, grilled over coals, served with nothing but lemon juice and parsley. Other steaks include *b~ alla pizzaiola* [pits-eye-**oh**-lah], with tomato and garlic and *b~ di filetto* [fee-**lay**-toh], rib steak.

When ordering steak, the following terms are important: *quasi cruda* [**kwah**-zee **kroo**-dah], nearly raw; *al sangue* [al **san**-gway], bloody; *a puntino* [poon-**teen**-oh], medium; *ben cotta* [ben **kot**-ah], well done.

Note that prices are often given *per etto* [**ett**-oh], one *etto* being 100g. Don't order a hearty 900g steak in the mistaken assumption that you will only pay the price quoted *per etto*!

bitter [**beet**-air] alcoholic or non-alcoholic sharp-flavoured aperitif.

bitto [**bee**-toh] a Lombard country cheese made from a mixture of goat's and cow's milk.

blecs [blecks] literally, 'patches of cloth', pasta from Friuli-Venezia Giulia resembling coarsely-cut patches.

blu [bloo] blue, often on menus denoting blue cheese.

blutnudeln [**bloot**-noo-deln] 'blood noodles', pasta from Trentino made from rye flour and pig's blood, served with sage and local cheese.

boba see BOGA.

boccale [bock-**ah**-lay] a jug or pitcher, usually for wine.

boccòn [bock-**on**] pasta from the Veneto traditionally made with RICOTTA cheese and spinach mixed into the dough.

bocconcino/i [bock-on-**chee**-noh] a bite-sized morsel(s), a little mouthful, something rather more formal and elaborately thought-out than an ASSAGGIO, used of delicate portions of stewed veal or fried rolls or balls of veal, ham, and cheese. The word can also be used to imply subtlety and delicacy in more substantial dishes, for example *bocconcini di vitello con funghi porcini e lamelle di tartufo bianco* is a veal stew with PORCINI and finely sliced white TRUFFLES. The veal is served in dainty mouthfuls. In cheese-making, *bocconcini* are the smaller balls of fresh MOZZARELLA: 'mouthfuls' as opposed to the standard size. The word has come to mean all bite-sized cheese rounds or ovals. *Bocconcini* is the diminutive of *bocconi*, which means mouthfuls. *Boccone squadrista*, the 'Airman's Titbit' was a Futurist recipe devised by Filippo MARINETTI consisting of a piece of fish served between two large apple slices, sprinkled with rum and set alight immediately prior to consumption.

boccone del prete [bock-**oh**-nay del **pray**-tay] 1. the 'priest's morsel', a choice cut in a stew reserved for the visiting local priest; 2. a kind of pork SALAME.

boffetto [boh-**fett**-oh] or *pan boffetto*, layers of toasted bread placed in a baking tray, interleaved with slices of roast chicken, cinnamon, sugar and cheese.

boga [**boh**-gah] bogue (fish; pl. *boghe*). Also called *boba*.

bogoni [bo-**goh**-nee] snails.

boldro [**bowl**-droe] frogfish or angler fish (Tuscany), see PESCATRICE.

Bolgheri [bol-**gay**-ree] wine-growing area of coastal Tuscany, home to some of the SUPERTUSCANS.

bollicine [boll-ee-**chee**-nay] bubbles in wine.

bollito/a [boll-**ee**-toh] boiled.

bollito misto [boll-**ee**-toh **mee**-stoh] a dish of mixed boiled meats, mainly sausages.

bologna [boll-**oh**-nya] a smooth, mild, often smoked, sausage.

Bolognese sauce the famous meat RAGÙ named after Bologna, its birthplace. It is typically eaten with an egg pasta such as TAGLIATELLE (purists will never eat it with spaghetti) and uses far less tomato in the preparation than commercial Bolognese sauces.

bomba di riso [**bom**-bah dee **ree**-zoh] a rice dish originating in Tuscany as a way of using up leftovers. The cooked rice is formed into a circular receptacle either by hand or by using a mould. The well in the middle is filled with meat and sauce, often pigeon, and then covered with a final layer of rice. The resulting 'bomb' is baked in the oven, turned out onto a dish and served.

bondiola [bon-dee-**oh**-lah] a spiced pork sausage from the province of Padua, Veneto.

bonito [bon-**ee**-toh] (or *bonita*), skipjack tuna.

bordatino [bor-da-**teen**-oh] a Tuscan soup with corn flour, beans, vegetables, and sometimes fish.

bordolese [bor-doh-**lay**-zay]

beef bone-marrow sauce, bordelaise.

borlengo [bor-**layn**-go] a flatbread, often eaten spread with PESTO MODENESE.

borlotti [bor-**loh**-tee] small red and pink speckled beans, often used in soups and stews and mostly bought dried.

borragine, borrana [borra-jee-nay, bor-**ah**-nah] borage, aromatic plant with edible blue flowers.

boscaiola, alla [bos-keye-**oh**-lah] with aubergine, mushrooms and tomato.

bosco [**boss**-koh] the woods, forest; *misto di bosco* is a dish of mixed wild berries.

botargo, bottarga [boh-**tar**-goh, boh-**tar**-gah] the salted and cured roe of grey mullet, popular in north and south. Regional variants are found in Sicily and the Veneto where it is served as an ANTIPASTO, thinly sliced and dressed with olive oil. *Bottarga* can be grated over pasta in the same way as truffles.

bottagio [bot-**adge**-oh] a stew.

See CASSOEULA.

botte [**bot**-eh] a cask or barrel for wine, as in the proverb *non si può avere la botte piena e la moglie ubriaca*: you can't have your barrel full and your wife drunk (you can't have your cake and eat it).

bottiglia [bott-**eel**-yah] bottle.

bovino [boh-**vee**-noh] beef.

bovoletto [boh-voh-**lay**-toh] a little snail.

bovoli [**boh**-voh-lee] snails.

Bra [brah] a cheese from Piedmont available in two varieties, *duro* (hard, and used for seasoning and grating in favour of the more expensive PECORINO) and *tenero* (soft and milder in taste).

bracciatelle [bratch-a-**tell**-ay] 'bracelets', ring-shaped loaves from Emilia-Romagna; also known as *brazadei* (brats-ah-**day**-ee).

brace, alla [**brah**-chay] cooked over embers.

Brachetto [brah-**ket**-oh] sweet Piedmontese red wine.

braciola [brah-**choh**-lah] a cutlet or chop, usually pork but may also describe lamb, beef, game and, sometimes, fish. The word is also used of a minute steak. *Braciola di maiale* is pork loin, served in Naples in a sauce made with tomatoes, garlic, capers and pine nuts. *Braciole*, in the plural, are chops.

bramangiare [brah-man-**jah**-ray] see BIANCOMANGIARE.

branxin [branx-**een**] in Venetian dialect, a sea bass.

branzi [**brant**-see] a fragrant alpine cheese from Bergamo, Lombardy.

branzino [brant-**see**-no] seabass, also known as *spigola*.

brasato [brah-**zah**-toh] a pot roast consisting of braised beef marinated in wine and braised with vegetables, often *al* BAROLO, i.e. with the red wine of that name. There are striking regional differences in flavour depending on the wine used.

brazadei see BRACCIATELLE.

bresaola [bray-**zah**-oh-lah] salted, air-dried beef, dark red in appearance, a speciality of Lombardy, but enjoyed across Italy; often served as an ANTI-PASTO, sliced thin and drizzled with olive oil and lemon. A SALUME.

bricchetti [brick-**ett**-ee] 'little sticks', pasta from Liguria served in MINESTRONE.

bringoli [**breen**-go-lee] 'twisted ones', pasta from Val di Pierle, Tuscany, served with a variety of local sauces.

brioche [bree-**osh**] a French term borrowed to describe a broad variety of semi-sweet breakfast pastries.

broccoletti, broccoli [bro-koh-**leh**-tee, **broh**-koh-lee] broccoli.

broccolo romanesco see ROMANESCO.

brodetto [broh-**det**-oh] soup, a diminutive of BRODO (broth) but nonetheless fairly substantial. *Brodetto di Pasqua* is chicken soup thickened with eggs and lemon, served at Easter in Florence and Lazio. In Italy's fishing ports, strikingly different fish-based *brodetti* have developed over the centuries, their ingredients dependant on what is readily available.

brodo [**broh**-doh] broth, a meat, poultry or fish stock, slowly reduced, often used as the basis for RISOTTO or heavier pasta dishes in which the pasta is cooked in the meat juices as opposed to being boiled in water.

brodo consumato [**broh**-doh con-zoo-**mah**-toh] clear chicken soup, consommé, also known as *brodo ristretto*.

brodosini [broh-doh-**zee**-nee] 'the watery, soupy ones' (pasta shapes), noodles served in broth, especially around Chieti in Abruzzo.

brodoso [broh-**doh**-zoh] runny, in a creamy, wholesome, slightly glutinous sense.

broeto [broh-**ayt**-oh] stock (Venetian dialect).

bros see BRUSS.

brossa [**bross**-ah] a runny RICOTTA, traditionally eaten with POLENTA, from Valle d'Aosta.

brovada [broh-**vah**-dah]

pickled turnips, fermented under grape marc (pressed skins, stems etc), then grated and cooked with a SOFFRITTO and vinegar, a speciality of Friuli-Venezia Giulia. *Brovada* is often served with FRICO cheese or MUSÈT, a typical Friulan sausage.

Brunello [broo-**nell**-oh] a clone of the SANGIOVESE grape grown around Montalcino in Tuscany. It produces one of Italy's finest DOCG wines.

bruscandoli [broos-**kan**-doh-lee] the shoots of the hop plant, used in soups and as a flavouring in sauces.

bruschetta [broos-**kay**-tah] toasted bread rubbed with garlic, drizzled with olive oil and garnished with tomatoes, onions and other toppings depending on the region or the imagination of the cook. Sometimes known as FETT'UNTA or PANUNTA in Tuscany and Umbria. See also CROSTINI and CROSTONI. *Bruschetta di fegatini* are *bruschetta* topped with sautéed chicken liver pieces, sometimes with a hint of chilli (PEPERONCINO).

bruss [broos] a pungent Piedmontese cheese spread made of fermented RICOTTA enlivened with pepper, herbs and sometimes chilli. Also known as *bros* or *brus*.

brustolini, bruscolini [broostoh-**lee**-nee, broos-koh-**lee**-nee] toasted pumpkin seeds.

brutti ma buoni [**broo**-tee mah **bwoh**-nee] 'ugly but good', almond biscuits.

bruzzo [**broo**-tsoh] fermented sheep's RICOTTA from the Ligurian alps.

bucaniera, alla [boo-kan-ee-**ay**-rah] 'pirate style', see CARRETTIERA.

bucatini [book-ah-**teen**-ee] 'pierced ones', hollow pasta strands, in eastern parts of Italy (Abruzzo, Marche) often served with a fish sauce. The best-known variant is *bucatini all'*AMATRICIANA, which takes its name from the town of Amatrice in northern Lazio.

bucato [book-**ah**-toh] 'pierced', the generic name for the many kinds of long pasta pierced down the centre, e.g. BUCATINI.

buccellati [bootch-ell-**ah**-tee] ring-shaped pastries filled with nuts and figs (Sicily).

buccellato [boo-chell-**ah**-toh] sponge cake with raisins, flavoured with aniseed. A speciality of Lucca, Tuscany.

buccuni [boo-**koo**-nee] see MURICE.

budella [boo-**dell**-ah] offal, intestines, the plural form of *budello*. In the Tuscan dish *budella alla sestese*, these are pig's intestines.

budellacci [boo-dell-**atch**-ee] (in Umbria) smoked, spiced pig intestines, usually spit-roasted or broiled.

budelletti [boo-dell-**ett**-ee] very thin intestines, either the real thing or pasta shapes. The latter are often served in PANCETTA-based sauces or, in Ascoli Piceno in the Marche, in a tuna sauce.

budino [boo-**deen**-oh] pudding; *budino di riso* is rice pudding; *budino di ricotta* is a soufflé with RICOTTA cheese, lemon and cinnamon.

bue [boo-ay] beef, a more colloquial word than the genteel *manzo*, as in a no-nonsense rural dish such as *bue brasato con gnocchi di polenta* (braised beef with polenta gnocchi).

bufalo, bufala [boo-fah-loh, boo-fah-lah] the water buffalo, the meat of which is eaten in some southern areas and whose milk is used for MOZZARELLA.

Bufalo, **the water buffalo**

Some say buffalo were introduced to Italy in the 6th century AD by the invading Goths, others that the Normans brought them to the mainland from Sicily c. AD 1000, still others that they were progressively introduced over time by pilgrims, crusaders and Arab merchants. They are hardy, versatile animals, having unusually large hooves that prevent them from sinking in muddy soil and therefore enable them to thrive in watery terrain. Though Neapolitan buffalo herds were slaughtered by the retreating Nazis during the Italian Campaign, the industry soon picked up after the Armistice. Buffaloes have an efficient digestive system that enables them to transform indifferent vegetation into protein-rich milk, high in mineral content and more nutritious than cow's milk.

---

bugie [boo-jee-ay] 'lies', Piedmontese nickname for a type of fried pastry made at Easter, the name alluding to the dishonest weakness of snacking on the sly during Lent.

buglossa [boo-**gloss**-ah] an edible leaf used in salads and soups; bugloss.

bukë [boo-kuh] ARBËRESH bread made with local hardgrain flour in antique woodburning furnaces, traditionally eaten with olive oil and RICOTTA.

buridda [boo-**ree**-dah] 1.

seafood stew (Liguria); 2. the Sardinian method of serving flat fish such as skate or ray cold, after simmering in stock and marinading in vinegar.

burrata [boo-**rah**-tah] a creamy cheese from Puglia, made from buffalo milk.

burrino [boo-**ree**-noh] a creamy, piquant, salted cheese, often filled with an inner core of butter, from Molise and Basilicata.

burro [**boo**-roh] butter.

burroso/a [boo-**roh**-zoh] buttery, ripe; *una pera burrosa*: a ripe ('buttery') pear.

busa, busiata [boo-**zah**, boo-zee-**ah**-tah] twisted pasta from Sardinia, made by winding a strand of dough around a thin stick or spike (the *busa*). *Busiata* is a robust Sicilian version of *busa*, described in the 15th-century *Libro de arte coquinaria* by Martino da Como, where he calls them '*maccaroni siciliani*': 'These *maccaroni* should be dried in the sun, and will last for two or three years, especially if done in the month of August; and cook them in water or meat broth; and put them on platters with a goodly quantity of grated cheese, fresh butter and sweet spices...' Today you can still find handmade *busiata* in Sicily, often served with *pesto alle sarde*, a sardine sauce.

busaki [boo-**zack**-ee] festive FETTUCCINE from Sardinia, served at Easter.

busara, alla [alla-boo-**zah**-rah] in a sauce of breadcrumbs, tomato, parsley, white wine and seasoning (Friuli-Venezia Giulia).

busecca [boo-**zeck**-ah] a thick tripe with vegetables and beans.

bussùl [boo-**sool**] the traditional short-stemmed shot-glass used for drinking GRAPPA.

caccia [**catch**-a] the hunt.

cacciagione [catch-a-**joe**-nay] game. If it has not been caught by the *cacciatore* then it will have been commercially farmed; in Italy game includes birds such as wood-cock, snipe and quail as well as large animals such as deer and the CINGHIALE, wild boar.

cacciatora, alla [alla-catch-a-**tore**-ah] 'hunter's style': cooked in a rich tomato sauce with mushrooms and sweet peppers.

cacciatorino [catch-a-tore-**ee**-noh] a small, hard SALAME, the name indicative of game content such as wild boar rather than domesticated meat.

cacciucco [catch-**ook**-oh] a fish stew of ancient Etruscan origin, native to Livorno, Tuscany. It is often noticeably *piccante* (spicy).

cacio [catch-oh] a southern term for cheese, as is the diminutive form *caciotta* [catch-**ot**-ah]. FORMAGGIO is the standard word but *cacio* is frequently used as a prefix. *Caciocavallo* is a southern Italian cow's milk cheese with a mild, slightly salty flavour. The name means 'horse cheese'; the cheeses are hung to mature over a pole known as the *cavallo* ('horse'). *Caciocavallo podolico* is a famously expensive cheese made exclusively from the milk of Podolica cows from Puglia. *Caciofiore aquilano* is cow's milk cheese scented with herbs and grasses, from L'Aquila (Abruzzo). *Cacio pepe* is a simple cheese and pepper pasta sauce. *Cacioricotta*, a piquant sheep's milk cheese, is produced in Puglia and often used for grating when it has matured. *Cacio raviggiolo* is fresh cheese (usually of cow's milk) from the Casentino region of northern Tuscany. First mentioned in the Middle Ages (a present of *cacio raviggiolo* was made to Pope Leo X in the 16th century), it is still produced as a niche product today.

cadunsei [cad-oon-**say**-ee] PASTA RIPIENA from Lombardy, a type of RAVIOLI filled with meat, salami, herbs and grated cheese, and, the *pièce de résistance*, an AMARETTO biscuit to give it crunch. Also known as *cahunei*, this is the traditional dish of the alpine valley of Val Camonica.

caffè [kah-**fay**] coffee.

Coffee in Italy: history and etiquette

Coffee first came to Italy around 1570, entering the port of Venice probably from Ottoman Istanbul. Pope Clement VIII (Ippolito Aldobrandini; 1536–1605) was an early and prominent Italian coffee enthusiast. It is said that when presented with a petition to ban the 'infidel' drink, he promptly 'baptised' a dish of coffee beans.

There are many different ways of making coffee in Italy, all of them falling into two categories: with milk (e.g. *cappuccino*) and without (e.g. *espresso*). Italians frown on the consumption of *cappuccino* after 11am, believing that coffee with milk is fine for breakfast but plays havoc with the digestion later in the day. Coffee may be ordered either *al banco* (at the bar) or *a tavola* (at the table). If drinking *al banco* you must first order and pay at the *cassa* (cash desk), then take the *scontrino* (receipt) to the bar and repeat your order, which you will then be given. If drinking *a tavola*, find a table or wait to be seated. Remember that table service costs more than service *al banco* for a good reason, and it is considered very *brutta figura* (ill bred) to pay bar prices and then surreptitiously attempt to sit down and finish your drink at a table.

A *bar* is an ordinary coffee bar but a *caffè* is something rather more exclusive, an elegant place, usually with a choice of inner, private rooms, and often with a history of famous patrons. Examples are Florian and Quadri in Venice, Pedrocchi in Padua, Giacosa in Florence and Caffè Greco in Rome.

Types of coffee

Espresso is the concentrated, brown-black potion brewed by forcing hot water under pressure through finely ground, roasted coffee beans. It is so called not because it is quick (which it usually is) but because it is made 'expressly' for the person who orders it. A *doppio espresso* or *caffè doppio* is a double *espresso* as opposed to a *caffè solo*, a single.

Ristretto means 'restrained', and a short shot of *espresso ristretto* is achieved by exposing the coffee grounds to hot water for fractionally less time, giving the caffeine less of a chance to intrude on the natural flavours of the coffee oils.

Caffè lungo, a 'long coffee' uses more water than a regular *espresso*, and the flavour is thus less intense.

Cappuccino is prepared with *espresso* and hot milk, the milk being steamed to a froth which gives the *cappuccino* its distinctive surface. It is named after the cowls of Capuchin monks. *Cappuccino senza schiuma* [**sen**-tsa skee-**oo**-mah] is *cappuccino* without too much foam and it is perfectly acceptable to ask for this: the *barista* will skim off a layer of *schiuma* with a knife.

Macchiato ('stained') is *espresso* 'stained' with a dribble of milk. You may also ask for a *latte macchiato* in which a generous slug of milk is 'stained' with a dash of coffee.

Caffè corretto means 'corrected' coffee, an *espresso* 'corrected' with a shot of GRAPPA, SAMBUCA or brandy. To specify which, order '*caffè corretto a grappa*' or '*corretto a sambuca*', or '*corretto a cognac*'. In simpler bars frequented by artisans you will encounter people, often market traders, drinking *corretto* at breakfast—it is not a good idea to emulate them unless you, too, have been at work since before dawn. An **ammazzacaffè** is a 'coffee killer', a small glass of liqueur drunk after coffee to dull its taste. There is a variation of this theme in the Veneto and Trentino, where it is customary to rinse out an empty coffee cup with grappa and pour the liquid into a glass. The resulting drink in known as a **resentin**, literally a 're-feeling' of the original coffee experience. In Piedmont this drink is known as **pussacaffè**.

An *americano* is black coffee prepared by adding hot water to *espresso*. *Caffè instantaneo* or *solubile* is instant coffee and to ask for it in an Italian bar would be a breathtaking solecism. *Caffè di cicoria* is chicory coffee or camp coffee, an acquired taste. *Bicerin* is a Torinese mixture of *cappuccino* and hot chocolate, sometimes served with whipped cream and decorated with chocolate powder. *Caffè alla turca* is Turkish coffee.

caglio [**kal**-yo] rennet, used to divide curds and whey in the cheese-making process.

cahunei [ca-hoon-**ay**-ee] see CADUNSEI.

caicc [ka-**eech**] PASTA RIPIENA from Lombardy with a filling of meat, greens and cheese.

cajubi [ka-**joo**-bee] short, worm-shaped pasta from Puglia, sometimes served in a soup but most usually *alla* RICOTTA.

Calabria [ka-**lah**-bree-ah] the peninsula forming the toe of Italy, site of the 7th-century BC Greek settlement of Sybaris, renowned for its citizens' devotion to the pursuit of pleasure. This ancient exuberance is annually reawoken at festival time, evident in the renowned and elaborate pastries and sweet RAVIOLI typical of the area. Famous Calabrian produce includes citrus fruits, aubergines (reputedly the finest in Italy) and onions (notably the red onions of Tropea). Its most highly-regarded wine is CIRÒ. It has lent its name to calabrese, a type of broccoli.

calamari [kalla-**mah**-ree] squid, not to be confused with the cuttlefish (*see illustrations on pp. 154–55*). *Calamari* (in the diminutive, *calamaretti*) are mainly deep fried or lightly boiled and served in seafood salads. Their black ink is used to flavour and colour both pasta and RISOTTO. *Calamari ripieni* are stuffed *calamari*; PROSCIUT-

TO CRUDO is a favourite filling. *Calamari in zimino* is a rich Tuscan stew of squid, garlic, spinach or chard, tomatoes and oil.

calcioni [kal-**chone**-ee] PASTA RIPIENA from the Marche, filled with RICOTTA and herbs. There is also a deep-fried, sweet version, dusted with sugar, the filling flavoured with lemon peel and cinnamon.

caldo/a [kal-doh] warm, hot.

calhù [kal-**hoo**] in Alpine dialect, 'trousers': PASTA RIPIENA from Lombardy, named after the traditional baggy breeches of the Val Camonica.

calia see SIMENZA.

calice [**kah**-lee-chay] wineglass.

calzoncelli [kalt-zon-**chay**-lee] traditional sweet pastries filled with RICOTTA, chestnut purée and/or chocolate.

calzone [kalt-**zone**-ay] 'trousers' or 'stockings'; in gastronomic terms a 'turnover', a crescent-shaped pasty with a savoury filling, often MOZZARELLA and tomato. In Sicily they are known as *cuddiruni* or *cudduruni*, and have a variety of fillings including onion, potatoes, broccoli and meat in addition to the usual cheese and tomato.

calzonicchi [kalt-**zoh**-nee-kee] pasta filled with brains, onions and spices, a delicacy of Roman Jewish cuisine.

camera [**kah**-may-rah] room, e.g. *servita nella sua camera*: served in your room.

camicia, in [in-ka-**mee**-chah] poached (lit. 'in a shirt').

camionista, alla [kam-ee-own-**east**-ah] 'lorry driver style', a term applied to a variety of robust dishes. See also CARRETTIERA.

camomilla [ka-moh-**mee**-lah] camomile.

camoscio [ka-**mosh**-oh] chamois.

campanelle [kampa-**nell**-ay] 'little bells', a pasta shape.

Campania [kam-**pah**-nee-ah] region of southern Italy, the location of important towns and cities including Naples,

Sorrento, Amalfi, Positano, Ravello and the islands Ischia and Capri. The region has been famous for its bounty since the days of the ancient Roman, who called it *Campania felix*, the 'happy land'. Campania is known for the quality of its fruit. The finest lemon trees are said to grow in and around Sorrento, traditional home of LIMONCELLO. Campania is also the land of PIZZA, which Naples claims to have invented. TAURASI is probably the region's finest red wine. Its most famous white is FIANO di Avellino.

Campanilismo, the key to Italy's regional diversity

Italy is a land of regions. This is obvious from the landscape, the architecture, political attitudes and linguistic variations. But nowhere is it more marked than in what you see on *trattoria* menus. Partly this diversity is a result of tradition. Today, however, when ingredients and ideas can and do travel great distances, regionalism owes its survival more to the will of the people and to their *campanilismo* [kam-pan-ee-**leez**-moh], 'bell-tower thinking', the belief that the *campanile* (bell-tower) of one's own town or village occupies the centre of the universe and that one's community produces the best cheese, wine and pasta in the world, has the prettiest girls, the handsomest men and the best restaurants. In gastronomic terms *campanilismo*, far from resulting in complacency and stagnation, is a vigorous commercial stimulant, each village, town, city, province and region competing with next for international recognition of its hospitality and produce.

Campari [kam-**pah**-ree]
a popular bitter aperitif, invented in the 19th century in Piedmont, by Gaspare Campari. It is usually served with soda and is also a key

ingredient of the popular NEGRONI cocktail.

campo [**kam**-poh] the countryside, a source of wild herbs and vegetables, e.g. *asparagi di campo*, wild asparagus.

candele [kan-**day**-lay] long, pierced pasta, similar to BUCATINI or ZITI (the larger versions).

canditi [kan-**dee**-tee] candied fruit.

canederli [kan-**ay**-dair-lee] bread dumplings, the Italian South Tyrolean version of Austrian and German *knödel*, a speciality of Trentino-Alto Adige. *Canederli* are made with stale bread mixed with milk and eggs, flavoured with a SOFFFRITTO of cheese or SPECK, onion and parsley. They are typically cooked and then served in meat broth.

canestrato pugliese [kan-eh-**strah**-toh poo-**lyay**-zay] Hard sheep's milk cheese with DOP status native to the province of Foggia in Puglia. The cheese is left to mature in traditional reed baskets (*canes-*

tre), the ribs of which give the rind its distinctive corrugated appearance. Sicilian PECORINO is sometimes called *canistratu* in dialect.

cannacce [kan-**atch**-ay] long pasta designed to resemble reeds, commemorating the burning at the stake of St Apollonia, patron saint of Ariccia in Lazio. On her feast day (9th Feb) a public feast is held where *cannacce* are served, along with other local delicacies, notably the town's famous SALSICCIA. *Cannacce* are very similar to (and sometimes also known as) ZITI.

cannariculi [kanna-**ree**-kool-ee] a Calabrian Christmas speciality: gnocchi-shaped pieces of dough, fried and then coated in honey or MOSTO COTTO. *Struffoli* and *cicirate* are other versions of the same thing.

cannella [kan-**ell**-ah] cinnamon.

cannellini [kan-ell-**een**-ee] white beans, similar in shape to kidney beans, bought dried and then soaked before being used in soups and stews.

cannelloni [kan-ell-**oh**-nee] large, tube-shaped pasta typically filled with minced meat or RICOTTA and spinach, and often topped with cheese or béchamel sauce. CRESPELLE are similar bu in pancake form. *Cannelloni alla partenopea* is a Neapolitan speciality, filled with a mixture of RICOTTA and MOZZARELLA and topped with tomato sauce.

cannizzu [kann-**eet**-zoo] in Sicily, a receptacle of woven reed, used for storing grain. It gives its name to a special bread, prepared on Christmas Eve and eaten to symbolise plenty in the coming year.

cannolicchi [kan-oh-**lee**-kee] 1. 'little tubes', a hollow pasta shape used in casseroles or vegetable soups; 2. razor clams. See CANNOLICCHIO.

cannolicchio [kan-oh-**lee**-kee-oh] the razor clam, a bivalve often cooked and served in one half of its shell with oil, garlic and parsley, garnished with lemon.

cannolo [**kan**-oh-loh] a Sicilian pastry cylinder filled with RICOTTA and flavoured with honey and vanilla.

Cannonau [kann-on-**ow**] Sicilian name for Grenache or Garnacha, the red-wine grape of Châteauneuf du Pape. As vinified in Sardinia, it is very dark in colour, and pleasingly rustic on the palate.

cannoncino [kan-on-**chee**-noh] a cream horn.

canoce [kan-**oh**-chay] (also *canocie*), Adriatic shrimps, also known as CICALE DI MARE.

canoe di mele [kan-**oh**-ay di **may**-lay] pastry 'canoes' filled with rum-laced cream and glazed apples. *Canoe salate* are the savoury version, with meat or fish fillings, slightly similar to a vol-au-vent.

cantarelli [kan-tah-**rell**-ee] fragrant yellow mushrooms; chanterelles. A native of beech and oak woods, they are found fresh in season (autumn) or dried. Also known as *finferli* or *gallinacci*.

cantucci, cantuccini [kan-**too**-chee, kan-too-**chee**-nee] hard, almond-flavoured biscuits that can be dipped into coffee or VINSANTO.

capelli d'angelo [kah-**pell**-ee **dan**-jel-oh] 'angel hair' pasta, so called because of its fine texture and appearance, in little curled bundles. It is also known as *capellini*.

capellini [ka-peh-**lee**-nee] 'little hairs', long pasta strands, thin, fine pasta often used in soups. Essentially a synonym for CAPELLI D'ANGELO.

capesante the scallop, seen in a variety of spellings including *cappasanta*. The scallop's other Italian names, *pellegrina* (pilgrim) and *conchiglia di San Giacomo* (St James's shell), allude to its religious symbolism. Pilgrims would often stitch a shell-shaped patch on their travelling capes before setting off for St James's major shrine in Spain, Santiago de Compostela. Many would carry shells as scoops, useful for helping oneself to the food provided by religious foundations along the route. Scallops are cooked in a variety of ways. They can be simmered simply with lemon and parsley, or served *au gratin*, with saffron sauce, or with pasta.

capicola see CAPOCOLLO.

caplaz see CAPPELLACCI.

capocollo [kap-oh-**kol**-oh] lit. 'head-neck', a dry-cured SALUME originating in Calabria (*Capocollo di Calabria* has DOP status). It is flavoured with different seasonings according to region. Similar to COPPA.

caponata [kap-oh-**nah**-tah] a rich, traditionally Sicilian, side dish, always made with aubergines, onions and tomatoes or tomato purée, and usually with capers, olives and celery as well. Other recipes call for pine nuts and peppers.

capone [kap-**pone**] 1. Sicilian name for LAMPUGA. *Capone apparecchiato* is *lampuga* in a sweet and sour sauce; 2. gurnard (fish).

cappa liscia [**kap**-ah **lee**-shah] the smooth Venus clam.

cappalunga [kap-ah-**loon**-gah] lit. 'long hat', the razor clam; see CANNOLICCHIO.

cappasanta [kap-ah-**san**-tah] see CAPESANTE.

cappellacci [ka-pel-**ah**-chee] 'little hats', a PASTA RIPIENA from Emilia-Romagna, particularly Ferrara, where they are known as *caplaz*. They are filled with a mixture of pumpkin, cheese and grated nutmeg. The dish is similar to TORTELLI *di zucca*.

cappelletti [ka-pel-**ett**-ee] small CAPPELLACCI; pasta 'hats', similar to TORTELLINI, stuffed with a variety of fillings, typically RICOTTA or PARMIGIANO REGGIANO. They are a speciality of Emilia-Romagna.

cappellini see CAPELLINI.

cappello del prete [ka-**pell**-oh del **pray**-tay] 'priest's hat': 1. a pork-meat sausage; 2. a shoulder cut of stewing beef.

capperi [**kapp**-er-ee] capers, the intensely-flavoured flower buds of the wild Mediterra-

Capesante or *cappaasanta*, the scallop.

nean shrub *Capparis spinosa*, usually preserved in vinegar or salt. The larger capers, often served on their stalks, pickled, with ANTIPASTI, are not the flower buds but the fruit.

cappon magro [kah-**pon mag**-roh] a Ligurian dish, a sort of seafood and vegetable trifle. The main ingredient is the CAPONE, though sometimes sea bass is used instead.

cappone [ka-**poe**-nay] 1. capon, a castrated rooster; 2. see CAPONE.

capra [**kap**-rah] goat, e.g. *formaggio di capra*: goat's cheese.

caprese [kap-**ray**-zay] in the style of Capri, commonly used of the simple salad

The artichoke (*carciofo*) is for some the quintessential Italian vegetable. It is particularly popular in Rome and in the Veneto.

insalata caprese, made with MOZZARELLA, tomato and basil.

capretto [ka-**pret**-oh] a kid, ideally a young milk-fed goat between 4 and 8 weeks old.

Capri [**kah**-pree] a large island off the coast of Campania, traditionally the favoured re-treat of sybarites and literati. Traditional Capri food is plain: cheese, pasta and fish, notably PEZZOGNA. The island gives its name to the CAPRESE salad.

capricciosa [ka-pree-**choh**-zah] the chef's 'caprice'.

caprini [ka-**pree**-nee] generic term for cheeses made with goat's milk, characterised by a strong flavour that becomes more pungent with maturity.

caprino degli Alburni [ka-**pree**-noh day-lee al-**boor**-nee] quick-maturing goat's milk cheese from Campania.

capriolo [kap-ree-**oh**-loh] roe buck venison.

carabaccia [karra-**batch**-ah] an onion soup occurring in many variations, sometimes with almonds and cinnamon. An ancient Tuscan dish.

carapigna [ka-ra-**peen**-ya] (Sardinia) a type of sorbet.

carasau [karra-**sa**-oo] thin sheets of Sardinian flatbread, traditionally eaten by shepherds when away from home with their flocks.

caratello [karra-**tell**-oh] a barrel (up to 200 litres capacity). *Caratelli* of 50 litres are traditionally used to make VINSANTO.

carbonara [kar-bon-**ah**-rah] pasta sauce made with diced ham, bacon or pig's cheek, cooked with garlic and then stirred into the pasta along with beaten eggs and PECORI-NO cheese (*see box opposite*).

The origins of *carbonara*

The sauce is said to take its name from the *carbonari*, the itinerant charcoal burners of Lazio and Abruzzo, who welcomed the hearty dish as a relief from their rigorous and lonely lifestyle. Others maintain it originated after WWII (it is unrecorded before then) as an Italian variant on the ham and eggs favoured by American soldiers. Another theory claims invention by, or in honour of, a secret society of 19th-century revolutionaries, known as the *Carbonari* because their quasi-masonic initiation rites bore similarities to charcoal-burning traditions. Upholders of this theory maintain that the recipe went unrecorded for so long because it had been veiled in secrecy to protect its originators. Yet another theory claims that *carbonara* is derives from the Austro-Czech *schinkenfleckerl*, a ham and pasta dish with a breadcrumb topping that found its way to Italy during the post-Napoleonic Habsburg era.

carbonata [kar-boh-**nah**-tah] see CARBONNADE.

carbonade [kar-boh-**nahd**] a rich beef and red wine stew from Valle d'Aosta, known as *carbonata* in the rest of Italy.

carbonizzato [kar-bon-it-**zah**-toh] chargrilled or barbecued.

carciofi [kar-**choff**-ee] artichokes, widely cultivated in Italy and found wild in many parts of Sicily and the south.

Older artichokes must be braised or boiled but young, tender specimens, known as *carciofini*, can be cut up and eaten raw in a salad or preserved in olive oil. *Carciofi alla giudea* (*or giudia*) are deep-fried, and typical of Roman Jewish cooking. *Carciofi alla romana* are served braised, stuffed with mint, garlic and breadcrumbs. *Carciofi alla*

veneziana are braised in oil
and white wine.

cardi [**kar**-dee] cardoons,
a vegetable related to the
thistle but actually part of
the artichoke family. The part
most used in cooking is the
stem. Cardoons are in season
in winter, and chopped stems
are typically found braised or
baked as a side dish or added
to soups and stews.

cardinale, alla [kar-dee-**nah**-
lay] 'cardinal style', in a white
sauce made with cream and
fish bouillon.

Cardini, Cesare (1896–1956)
Italian-Mexican restaurateur,
inventor of the Caesar Salad.
The salad is named after Mr
Cardini, not after one of the
Roman emperors as is some-
times supposed.

carnaroli [kar-nah-**rohl**-ee] a
medium-grain rice from Lombardy, used for RISOTTO.

carne [**kar**-nay] meat, e.g.
carne ai ferri (grilled meat),
carne cruda (raw meat), *carne
di maiale* (pork), *carne di manzo* (beef), *carne ovina* (sheep,

lamb or mutton). *Carne cruda
all'Albese* is steak tartare with
truffle sauce, the *albese* alluding to Alba, the truffle capital
of Italy (see TARTUFO). *Carne
di cavallo* or *carne equina* is
horse meat.

carne salada [**kar**-nay sal-
ah-dah] salt beef, a speciality
of Trentino-Alto Adige. It is
either eaten cold, or as a hot
dish with BORLOTTI beans:
carne salada e fasoi.

caro [**kahr**-oh] caraway.

carota [kar-**oh**-tah] carrot,
along with onions and celery
one of the 'Holy Trinity' of
Italian cooking. See SOFFRITTO.

carpa [**kar**-pah] carp.

carpaccio [kar-**patch**-oh]
originally, thin-sliced raw beef
(*see box opposite*) with mayonnaise dressing, now widely
used for any thin-sliced raw
meat or fish served with
either a vinaigrette or olive
oil and shavings of PARMESAN
or similar cheese. In order to
slice the meat to the required
wafer-thinness, the meat must
be cold and the knife sharp.

The invention of *carpaccio*

Beef *carpaccio* is said to have been invented in 1950 by Giuseppe Cipriani, founder of Harry's Bar in Venice. He devised it for Countess Amalia Nani Mocenigo, who had been advised by her doctor to eschew cooked meat. Today's champions of Raw Foodism, also known as the Palaeolithic Diet, would have applauded. Raw products, after all, give stimulus to the digestive enzymes: anyone who embraces the diet can hope to recapture the get-up-and-go spirit of their cave-dwelling forebears. Cipriani added sophistication to this raw elementality with a mustard mayonnaise and then completed the effect by naming it after the 16th-century Venetian painter Vittore Carpaccio, whose gentle and luminous palette, dominated by cream and red, are echoed in the tints of the raw meat and mayonnaise.

carpione [kar-pee-**oh**-nay] 1. freshwater fish native to two Italian lakes, Garda and Posta Fibreno (Lazio). Both species are endangered; 2. a marinade: *in carpione* means soused in wine and vinegar, e.g. *zucchini in carpione*.

carrettiera, alla [karr-et-ee-**ay**-rah] 'cart-driver style' in reference to a simple, hearty spaghetti sauce. Various recipes exist: tuna and cheese are staple ingredients; tomatoes, mushrooms and chilli are sometimes added. Compare BUCANIERA and ZAPPATORA.

carsenta lunigianese [kar saint-ah loo-nee-jah-**nay**-zay] a Tuscan bread, traditionally baked on a fire of chestnut leaves.

carta da musica [**kar**-tah da **moo**-zee-kah] a large, circular, thin, crisp flatbread some 40cm (16 inches) in diameter, resembling an outsized poppadum and similar to the Sardinian CARASAU. The name, 'music sheet', is a reference to its unusual size and paper-thin consistency, though its antecedents may be rooted even more deeply in antiquity. Virgil refers to the *orbem fatalis crusti* (*Aeneid* VII:115), the circular flatbreads 'of destiny', eaten by Aeneas and his men when they disembarked at Italy for the first time, in what today is Lazio. These were very likely the forebears not only of today's *carta da musica* but of all other circular flatbreads and *pizze* in Italy.

cartellate [kar-tell-**ah**-tay] thin strips of puff pastry from Puglia, fried in oil and often coated with honey.

cartoccio [kar-**totch**-oh] parchment, used to wrap meat and especially fish, together with herbs and vegetables, prior to baking. *Cartoccio di pesce spada* = swordfish baked in this way.

carvi [**kahr**-vee] caraway.

casalinga [kah-zah-**leen**-gah] a housewife; *cucina casalinga* [koo-**chee**-nah kah-sah-**leen**-gah] is home cooking.

casarecce [kah-zah-**ray**-chay] also known as *cesariccia*, short lengths of pasta resembling a rolled and twisted tube or scroll.

casatiello [kah-zah-tee-**ell**-oh] a Neapolitan Easter pie with a filling of PARMESAN and PECORINO cheese, eggs, SALAME, PANCETTA and pepper.

casciotta d'Urbino [kash-**ott**-ah door-**been**-oh] soft cheese from the Marche, made of a mixture of sheep and cow's milk. At the time of writing it was the Marche region's only DOP product.

Casella, Cesare (b.1960) Tuscan-born chef, Dean of Italian Studies at the Italian Culinary Academy in New York. His company Republic of Beans has done much to popularise Italian food in the USA. He helped set up a project to raise Italian breeds of cattle and pigs on farms in upstate New York. He is the author of a number of cookbooks.

casereccio/a [kah-zeh-**retch-**

oh] home-made; of bread, home-baked. Applied to any food it suggests comfort, wholesomeness and mother's cooking.

casieddu [ka-zee-**ed**-oo] a goat's cheese from Moliterno (Basilicata) that owes its distinctive flavour to the ferns through which the milk is filtered and to the catmint (*nepeta*) which is added to it.

casolèt [kah-zoh-**let**] a soft, mild cow's milk cheese from Trentino.

cassa [**kass**-ah] the cash desk in a bar or café.

cassata [kass-**ah**-tah] 1. a rich cake with alternate layers of liqueur-moistened sponge and sweetened RICOTTA cheese, covered with an outer carapace of marzipan icing traditionally decorated with green and pink stripes and topped with candied fruit; 2. a Neapolitan ice cream containing candied fruit.

cassateddi, cassatelli [kassa-**tedh**-ee, kassa-**tell**-ee] sweet *ricotta* turnovers (Sicily).

Casarecce, short pasta twisted in order to catch and retain the sauce.

cassoeula [kas-oh-**oo**-lah] a Milanese winter stew of cheap cuts of pork and cabbage. Also known as *bottagio*.

cassola [kass-**oh**-lah] 1. a thick pancake characteristic of Jewish cuisine, made by beating RICOTTA with eggs and sugar. The pancake mix is fried in olive oil until brown on both sides; 2. in Sardinia, a fish stew.

cassulli [kass-oo-lee] Sardinian *gnocchi* traditionally served *alla carlofortina*, with a basil and tomato sauce.

castagna [kass-**tan**-ya] chestnut; also known as *marrone* [mah-**roh**-nay]; important in Tuscan, Ligurian and Sardinian cuisine, extensively used either fresh or milled into flour. Fresh chestnuts may poached in wine, roasted, or fried in butter as a garnish. Candied chestnuts are popular in Piedmont.

castagnaccio [kass-tan-**yatch**-oh] a sweet, chestnut-flour flatbread from Tuscany.

castagnole [kass-tan-**yoh**-lay] chestnut-shaped balls of sweet pastry laced with rum or other liqueur.

Castel Ariund [kas-**tell** arry-**oond**] full-flavoured cow's milk cheese from Piedmont, ideally eaten with honey.

Castelluccio [kas-tell-**oo**-choh] village on the border of Umbria and the Marche known for its lentils.

castrato [kass-**trah**-toh] a young sheep that has been castrated.

castraure [kass-trah-**ooh**-ray] the first buds of artichokes that grow in the Venetian lagoon, pruned to encourage the plant to produce an abundant crop. They are very tender and tasty, and can be eaten raw or lightly braised.

Cavalcanti, Ippolito, Duca di Buonvicino (1787–1859), Neapolitan author of *Cucina teorico pratica* (*The Theory and Practice of Cuisine*, 1837), a collection of 600 recipes with an inner core of Neapolitan favourites written in dialect.

cavallucci [kav-ah-**loo**-chee] Sienese almond biscuits, from *cavalli* ('horses'), supposedly referring to an ancient tradition in which employers supplied coach hands and stable lads with similar biscuits.

cavatappi [ka-vah-**tap**-ee] pasta corkscrews.

cavatelli [ka-vah-**tell**-ee] type of pasta curled over to catch the sauce. Also known as *cavatieddi*. A traditional way to serve them is *con la* RUCOLA.

cavatieddi see CAVATELLI.

cavedano [ka-vay-**dah**-noh] a freshwater fish, the chub. Good for frying, breading and poaching.

caviale [kah-vee-**ah**-lay] caviar.

cavolata [kah-voh-**lah**-tah] cabbage soup.

cavoletti see CAVOLINI.

cavolfiore [kah-vol-fee-**ore**-ay] cauliflower.

cavolini di Bruxelles [kah-voh-**lee**-nee dee broo-**sell**] Brussels sprouts, also known as *cavoli* or *cavoletti*.

cavolo [**kah**-voh-loh] cabbage, much used in winter soups. Popular varieties include the *cavolo nero*, the dark-leaved cabbage of Tuscany.

cavolo broccolo [**kah**-voh-loh **brock**-oh-loh] broccoli, particularly the pale green, pointy kind.

cavolo con le fette [**kah**-voh-loh con lay **fay**-tay] 'cabbage with slices': toasted bread with oil and garlic, topped with warm Tuscan cabbage.

cazzaregli [cats-a-**ray**-lyee] in Molise, STROZZAPRETI.

cazzellitti [cats-ell-**ee**-tee] gnocchi-like pasta from Abruzzo.

cazzilli [cats-**eel**-ee] potato croquettes.

cecamariti [chay-kah-mah-**ree**-tee] 'husband blinders', food so delicious that it blinds a husband to the misdemeanours of his wife. In Puglia the term refers either to a kind of pasta or to a rich pea soup.

cecatelli [chay-kah-**tell**-ee] short pasta, similar in shape to CAVATELLI.

ceci [**chay**-chee] chickpeas.

cecina [**chay**-chee-nah] chickpea bread from Volterra, Tuscany.

cecinelli [chay-chee-**nell**-ee] 1. small chickpeas; 2. in Naples, smelt, small fish.

cedro [**chay**-droh] citron, a large citrus fruit resembling a monster lemon. Also known as *citro* to avoid confusion with the word for a cedar tree or cedar wood, which is also *cedro*.

cefalo [**chay**-fah-loh] grey mullet.

cena [**chay**-nah] dinner, supper, evening meal.

cenci [**chen**-chee] deep-fried pastries, fritters.

cencioni [chen-**chone**-ee] 'little rags', a pasta shape, either in strips or ovals.

centerbe [chain-**tair**-bay]

vivid green herbal DIGESTIVO from Abruzzo made by macerating a variety of herbs and plants (the name means '100 herbs') in alcohol.

centopelli [chayn-toh-**pell**-ee] see OMASO.

cerasa [che-**rah**-za] cherry.

Cerasuolo di Vittoria [chay-rah-**swoh**-loh dee vee-**toh**-ree-ah] DOCG red wine from southern Sicily.

cerfoglio [chair-**foh**-lyoh] chervil.

cernia [**chair**-nee-ah] grouper (saltwater fish).

cervellata [chair-vell-**ah**-tah] a Calabrian pork SALAME.

cervello [chair-**vell**-oh] brain (pl. *cervelli*).

Cervio, Vincenzo

Carver-in-chief (*trinciante*) to Cardinal Alessandro Farnese in Rome. His 1582 treatise on carving, *Il trinciante*, established him as the high priest of theatrical table service, revealing the elaborate ceremonial of his craft and the stamina required to practise it successfully. The elaborately liveried carver, prominently in sight of high table, would secure the heavy joint of meat on a dagger or trident and hold it aloft at arm's length above the carving dish. Then, often to an orchestral or choral accompaniment, he would bestow horizontal and vertical slashes to the surface of the flesh, a final *coup de grâce* resulting in a cascade of morsels onto the dish below. Whilst Cervio was the acknowledged master, the first treatise on the Italian art of carving was the *Refugio del povero gentilhuomo* (*The Refuge of Poor Gentlemen*, 1520) by Giovanni Francesco Colle, *trinciante* to the Court of Ferrara. The title reflects the tradition that master-carvers were frequently men from noble families who had fallen on hard times. Cervio was unusual in that he began as a menial in the court of Urbino, working his way up to be steward and later master-carver.

cervo [**chair**-voh] stag, venison. *Noce di cervo* is rump of venison. *Spezzatino di cervo* is venison stew.

cespo [**chess**-poh] a head of lettuce.

cestello, cestino, cestinetto [chess-**tell**-oh, chess-**tee**-noh, chess-tee-**nett**-oh] a small basket. A *cestino/cestinetto di verdure* is a serving (in a little basket or similar) of vegetables.

cetriolo [chet-ree-**oh**-loh] cucumber (pl. *cetrioli*). *Cetriolini* are pickled cucumbers, gherkins.

cheppia [**kep**-ee-ah] a freshwater fish similar to the herring, also known as *alosa*.

chiacchiere [kyah-**kyay**-ray] 'chatterers', festive fried pastries, strips or ribbons of fried or baked pastry, often cut with a zigzag ('pinked') edge, and dusted with powdered sugar, a favourite at carnivals. They go by a variety of names according to region, including *fiocchetti* ('little bows'), *frappe*, *cenci* and *bugie*.

chiancaredde [kee-ann-ka-**red**-ee] flattened chunks of pasta from Puglia, somewhat resembling coins. The Taranto-born photographer and writer Lorenzo Manigrasso has written a hymn in their honour, where he speaks of the 'generations of hands' who have made them, and of the 'humble value of an existence when computers didn't exist'. Also *chiancarelle*.

Chianina [kya-**nee**-nah] breed of cattle from the Val di Chiana region of Tuscany. They supply the beef used in the traditional BISTECCA *alla fiorentina*.

Chianti Classico [kee-**ann**-tee **class**-ee-koh] wine-growing area between Siena and Florence, whose producers may use the GALLO NERO emblem on their labels. Chianti is the most famous wine of Tuscany, a youthful red, made mainly or entirely from the SANGIOVESE grape. If other grapes are added to the blend, these may only (since a ruling of 2006) be red-wine grapes. Earlier wines which used white MALVASIA would not now qualify as Chianti Classico. TIGNANELLO is a famous wine made in the Chianti region, though it does not label itself a Chianti.

Chianti Rufina [kee-**ann**-tee roo-**fee**-nah] respected Tuscan winery lying outside the boundaries of the Chianti Classico area that brought Chianti to the international scene in traditional straw-covered bottles. These flasks, that would have been slung across the saddles of medieval hunters and warriors, were widely seen in *trattorie* in the UK and USA throughout the '60s and '70s. Once the wine was finished, the bottles often enjoyed an afterlife as candlesticks, the straw jacket becoming ever more encrusted with trickling wax.

chiarello [kya-**rell**-oh] light-coloured red wine.

chiaretto [kya-**ret**-oh] pale red wine.

chiccara [kee-kahr-ah] a cup. The name derives from the Spanish *jícara*, a drinking gourd.

chicco [kee-koh] a grain, a (coffee) bean.

chifferi [kee-fer-ee] small, curved, tubular PASTA CORTA widespread in Italy, named after the *Kipferl*, the little Austrian pastry it resembles.

chinulille [kin-oo-**leel**-ay] sweet RAVIOLI served at Christmas and other feasts (Calabria). Also known as *chinuliddri*.

chiocciole [kee-**otch**-oh-lay] 1. snails; 2. snail-shaped pasta, also known as PIPE.

chiodi [kee-**oh**-dee] cloves.

chitarrine [kee-tar-**ee**-nay] slender noodles made on the *chitarra*, a board strung with wires like a guitar. Also known as *pasta alla chitarra*. When coloured with squid ink, they are *chitarrine nere*.

chiummenzana, alla [kyoo-mayn-**tzah**-nah] tomato-and-herb pasta sauce from Capri and the Amalfi Coast.

chiuso [kyoo-zoh] closed, for a variety of reasons including: *per ferie* (for the holidays); *per restauro* (for restoration); *per lutto* (due to bereavement); *per ristrutturazione* (for redevelopment); *per motivi di sicurezza* (for security reasons); *per azione sindacale* (because of industrial action).

chivarzu [kee-vart-zoo] coarse-textured bran loaves (Sardinia).

ciabatta [cha-bah-tah] lit. 'the carpet slipper'; internationally popular bread with a crisp crust and a soft interior with air pockets (*see box below*).

Loafing in the fast lane: the story of *ciabatta*

The *ciabatta* was the brainchild of Arnaldo Cavallari, a retired rally driver from the Veneto who later took over his family's flour mills in Adria. By the early '80s, Cavallari had become alarmed at what he saw as disproportionately high imports of French bread, especially baguettes, into Italy. In his days as a rally driver Cavallari had shown the rest of Europe, including the French, that he was a force to be reckoned with. In 1966, for example, he and Dante Salvay had conclusively won the Mitropa Rally Cup, speeding to victory in their Alfa Romeo Giulia GTA. Determined to apply the unwavering spirit of the race track to the ovens of the Veneto, in 1982 Cavallari patented the *ciabatta*. The shrewdly-judged act of entrepreneurial patriotism paid off richly and today the *ciabatta* is famous all over the world. As to variations on the original theme, *ciabatta integrale* is made with wholemeal flour, while *ciabatta al latte* is the result of adding milk to the dough. Ciabatta dough has many regional seasonings and the possibilities are nearly infinite. Romans favour a simple formula of olive oil, salt, and marjoram. Small, filled *ciabatte* are the archetypal quick lunch.

ciaccia [**cha**-cha] in Tuscany, a FOCACCIA, also known as *schiacccia, schiacciata.*

cialda [**chal**-dah] a fine crisp or wafer, a waffle.

ciambella [cham-**bell**-ah] a ring-shaped cake or loaf.

ciambotta, cianfotta [cham-**bot**-ah, chan-**fot**-ah] vegetable stew with potatoes, tomatoes, aubergine, onion, and peppers.

ciapinabò [cha-pee-nah-**bo**] Jerusalem artichoke.

ciarduna [char-**doon**-ah] a sweet Sicilian pastry with a RICOTTA or MASCARPONE filling.

ciauscolo [**chow**-skohl-oh] a soft spreadable SALAME typical of the Marche, made from the belly and shoulder of pork with half the weight again in pork fat, the mixture well seasoned, stuffed into an intestine, smoked in juniper wood and then air-dried.

cibo [**chee**-boh] food.

cibreo di rigaglie [chee-**bray**-oh dee ree-**gah**-lyay] chicken livers and cock's combs fried in butter, then simmered in a broth thickened with egg yolks and lemon.

cicale di mare [chick-**ah**-lay-di-**mah**-ray] mantis shrimps, popular in the Venice region.

cicatelli see CECATELLI.

cicc [cheek] fried buckwheat FOCACCIA from Lombardy.

ciccheti [chee-**kay**-tee] savoury bar snacks (Venice).

ciccioli [**chee**-choh-lee] crispy fragments of pork fat. Also called *siccioli* [**seech**-oh-lee].

cicerchiata [chee-chair-kee-**ah**-tah] traditional cake of Abruzzo and Molise, in the form of a ring or mound of fried dough balls.

cicerchie [chee-**chair**-kee-ay] the seeds of the chickling vetch, a legume from Central Italy. Once a popular peasant food, it is now more difficult to find. The seeds look very much like chickpeas and are used in a similar way, in soups and stews.

ciceri e tria [**chee**-chay-ree eh **tree**-ah] pasta with chickpeas (Puglia). The ancient Roman orator Cicero got his name from the fact that one of his ancestors is said to have had a nose shaped like a chickpea.

cicione [chee-**choh**-nay] a small GNOCCHI-shaped pasta from Sardinia, resembling a chickpea and coloured and flavoured with saffron.

cicirate see CANNARICULI.

cicoria [chick-**oh**-ree-ah] chicory. The leaves are used for salads or are boiled and served as a side dish or in soups and stews. The roots are ground up and used as a coffee substitute or additive.

ciliegie [chilly-**ay**-jay] cherries.

cima [**chee**-mah] a Ligurian speciality (generally known as *cima alla genovese*) consisting of a thin cut of veal formed into a pocket and stuffed with a mixture of vegetables, pine nuts and cheese. The pocket is tightly sewn and boiled. It is served in slices, either hot or cold.

cime di rapa [**chee**-may dee **rah**-pah] turnip tops, the leaves of field mustard (*Brassica rapa*). They have a pleasant, nutty flavour and are often sautéed with garlic and olive oil and served over pasta, typically ORECCHIETTE.

cinesi rigati [chee-**nay**-zee ree-**gah**-tee] ridged pasta, similar to CONCHIGLIE.

cinghiale [cheen-**gyah**-lay] the wild boar, popular in northern and central Italy, particularly Tuscany, and cooked in a variety of ways. *Cinghiale in agrodolce* (in sweet and sour sauce) is cooked with herbs and spices such as ginger and cloves; *cinghiale alla cacciatora* is wild boar 'huntsman style', simmered slowly in white wine with onion, carrot and parsley. Wild boar sausages are also made during the hunting season.

cinta senese [**cheen**-tah say-**nay**-zay] an ancient breed of long-haired Tuscan pig (literally 'the Sienese belt') that narrowly escaped extinction in the European agricultural reforms of the 1980s. A small but meticulously reared cluster of herds now thrives in the Tuscan countryside, little changed in appearance since the 14th century when they were depicted by the Sienese artist Ambrogio Lorenzetti in his cycle of frescoes *Gli Effetti del Buon Governo* (Siena, Palazzo Pubblico). Here a stalwart little black pig, with the distinctive broad white band around its middle and down the foreleg, is seen being used as a truffle-hunter. Today, the breed is highly prized; the black hind hooves are often left untrimmed on the finished PROSCIUTTO as a mark of authenticity.

Cinzano a popular aperitif, a vermouth flavoured with a blend of herbs and spices, created in the mid-18th century in Turin by the Cinzano brothers. Cinzano Rosso was the original type; since then Cinzano Bianco, Cinzano Extra Dry and Cinzano Rosé have appeared.

ciocchetti [chock-**ett**-ee] a curled, tube-shaped pasta.

cipolla [chee-**poh**-lah] onion (pl. *cipolle*).

cipollaccio [chee-poh-**latch**-oh] also known as *lampascioni* [lam-pash-**oh**-nee], these are grape-hyacinths, with an onion-like edible bulb.

cipolline [chee-poll-**ee**-nay] spring onions.

Cipriani, Giuseppe (1900–80) inventor of CARPACCIO and founder of Harry's Bar in Venice.

cipudduzzi [chee-poo-**doot**-see] the bulbs of grape-hyacinths, see CIPOLLACCIO.

ciriola romana [**cheery**-oh-lah roh-**mah**-nah] a bread roll typical of Rome, so called because its elongated shape is supposedly reminiscent of a type of young eel (*ciriola*) once fished in the Tiber.

ciriole [cheery-**oh**-lay] 1. 'little eels', spaghetti-type pasta typical of Umbria, where it is prepared *alla Ternana* (with garlic and chilli) or *alla norcina* (with truffles); 2. young eels, a speciality of Lazio, steamed in white wine with peas. Recipes usually call for live eels, since their flesh (like that of most oily fish) deteriorates more rapidly than other varieties. Eels are known to put up a fight and leap from the pan.

Cirò [chee-**ro**] town in Calabria which prides itself on its wine tradition, one of the oldest in the world. Both red and white wine is made. The reds are tannic and fruity, made largely from the Gaglioppo grape.

ciufele [**choo**-fay-lay] a type of pasta from Molise, similar to CAVATELLI.

ciuppin [choo-**peen**] a hearty fish stew (Liguria). There is no set recipe: whatever the boats had brought in, or any fish left over at the end of market day, would be used, cooked together with tomatoes and other vegetables.

civreo [chee-**vray**-oh] see CIBRÈO.

cjalsons [kee-al-**sons**] 'trousers' in local dialect, PASTA RIPIENA from Friuli-Venezia Giulia, made with a variety of fillings, typically RICOTTA and spinach and served with melted butter. Also known as *cjarsons*.

clementino [klay-mayn-**teen**-oh] seedless mandarin orange.

cobeletti [koh-be-**lay**-tee] (also *gobeletti*), Ligurian jam tarts, traditionally served on 5th Feb, the feast of St Agatha, patron saint of bakers.

cocciolette see ABISSINI.

cocco, noce di cocco [**koh**-koh, **noh**-chay dee **koh**-koh] coconut.

cocomero [koh-koh-**may**-roh] in southern Italy, a watermelon.

cocuzza [koh-**koot**-sah] regional word for a pumpkin or squash; can also mean a person's head or 'nut', e.g. *la moglie* (his wife) *ha colpito* (bashed) *la sua cocuzza* (his nut) *con un mattarello* (with a rolling pin).

coda [**koh**-dah] tail. *Coda alla vaccinara* is oxtail stew, literally 'the tail' (*coda*) cooked in the manner of the *vaccinaro* (butcher). In ancient times and well into the Middle Ages it was customary to pay the butcher in kind by allowing him the hide, entrails and tail of the animal.

coda di rospo [**koh**-dah dee **ros**-poh] monkfish, literally 'toad's tail'. *Coda di rospo fumegada* is a Venetian speciality where the fish is soused in a black pepper marinade and wrapped in smoked PANCETTA before being roasted or grilled.

coffee see CAFFÈ.

coj [cozh] Piedmontese dialect for cabbage.

cojette [cozh-**ett**-ay] GNOCCHI from Piedmont made with flour, stale bread, milk and aromatic herbs.

colazione [kol-at-see-**own**-ay] a meal, usually breakfast, which is correctly *prima colazione*, the 'first' meal.

colla de pesce [**kol**-ah dee **pay**-shay] sheet gelatin.

colomba pasquale [kol-**om**-bah pas-**kwah**-lay] a dove-

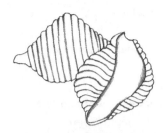

Conchiglie, pasta shells.

shaped Easter loaf (*colomba* = 'dove') from Lombardy, studded with sugar and almonds.

colombaccio [kol-om-**batch**-oh] wood pigeon.

comino [koh-**mee**-noh] see CUMINO.

companatico [kompa-**nah**-tee-koh] (pl. *companatici*) something to accompany bread, e.g. olives or SALUME.

composta [kom-**poss**-tah] a *compôte*, usually of fruit.

composto [kom-**poss**-toh] a mixture, a blend.

con, col with.

concentrato [kon-chen-**trah**-toh] a concentrate or purée.

conchiglie [kon-**kee**-lee-ay] shell-shaped pasta widespread throughout Italy. Also known as *conchigliette*.

conchiglioni [kon-kee-lee-**own**-ee] the larger version of *conchiglie*, enormous pasta shells with a distinctive grooved surface.

condigiun, condiglione [kon-dee-**joon**, kon-dee-**lyoh**-nay] a substantial Ligurian salad, in some ways resembling a *salade niçoise*, made with tomatoes, cucumber, black olives, basil, garlic, anchovies, hard boiled egg, oregano and tuna.

condimento [kon-dee-**mayn**-toh] a condiment, dressing or seasoning.

confetti di pistoia [kon-**fet**-ee dee pee-**stoy**-ah] aniseed comfits named after the town of Pistoia, Tuscany.

confettura [kon-fet-**oo**-rah] jam, also called *marmellata*. If in need of marmalade, ask for *confettura di arancia* or *marmellata di arancia*.

confortini [kon-for-**teen**-ee] little biscuits, typically made of hazelnut and aniseed.

congelato/a [kon-jel-**ah**-toh] frozen.

coniglio [kon-**eel**-yoh] rabbit.

conservanti [con-sair-**van**-tee] preservatives.

contenuto calorico [kon-tay-**noo**-toh kal-**oh**-ree-koh] calorific content, e.g. *piatti con moderato contenuto calorico* (moderate-calorie dishes).

contorno [kon-**torn**-oh] side dish (pl. *contorni*).

controfiletto [**kon**-troh-fee lay-toh] sirloin, entrecôte.

coperto [koh-**pair**-toh] the cover charge for a meal, covering the cost of bread and water.

coppa [**koh**-pah] 1. a salted, cured sausage made from the neck or shoulder of pork and often sliced for use in sandwiches or as an ANTI-PASTO. Varieties include: *coppa di Parma* and *coppa piacentina* (from Piacenza); 2. a cup, e.g. *coppa di gelato*, ice cream in a cup.

coppiette [koh-pee-**ett**-ay] salted dried strips of meat, typically beef.

coque, uovo alla [**kok**-way] soft-boiled egg.

coralli, corallini [koh-**rah**-lee, koh-rah-**lee**-nee] tiny sections of pasta tube widespread in Italy, named after the beads in a coral necklace.

coratella d'agnello [koh-rah-**tell**-ah dan-**yell**-oh] lamb's offal.

corbezzola [core-**bets**-oh-lah] arbutus, tree-strawberry (pl. *corbezzole*).

corbo [**kor**-boh] see CORVINA.

cordelle [kor-**dell**-ay] pasta 'ropes'. Long pasta similar to LINGUINE.

coregone [koh-reg-**oh**-nay] whitefish, freshwater fish found in the lakes, especially Lake Garda.

coriandolo [koh-ree-an-**doh**-loh] coriander.

cornetto [core-**nay** toh] 1. croissant; 2. *Cornetto de mà*, see MURICE.

corniola [kor-nee-**oh**-lah] the dogwood or cornel cherry, a bitter fruit used to make relishes and meat sauces in northern Italy.

corno di bue [**kor**-noh dee **boo**-ay] 'ox horn', *peperoni*

corno di bue are sweet yellow or red peppers from Carmagnola in Piedmont. Excellent for stuffing.

corposo [kor-**poh**-zoh] full-bodied (wine).

corto [**kor**-toh] 1. short; 2. a *ristretto*, see CAFFÈ.

Corvina [kor-**veen**-ah] red grape which along with Rondinella and MOLINARA is used to produce the wine of the Lake Garda region, notably the famous VALPOLICELLA.

corvina [kor-**veen**-ah] the corb fish, cooked in the same manner as sea bass, also known as *corvo*, *corbo* or *ombrina*.

corzetti [cort-**set**-ee] thin, circular pasta 'coins' from Liguria embossed with patterns (traditionally made by carved wooden stamps) including flower motifs and family coats of arms.

cosacavaddu [koh-zah-kah-vah-**dhoo**] a pungent Sicilian cow's milk cheese.

coscia [**kosh**-a] in anatomy, the thigh. As a cut of meat, the leg, e.g *coscie di rana* (frog's legs) or *coscia di pollo* (chicken drumstick). Also known as *cosciotto* [kosh-**ott**-oh], as in *cosciotto d'agnello*, a leg of lamb.

costa, costata [**kos**-tah, kos-**tah**-tah] 1. a chop, e.g. *costa di maiale alla griglia*: grilled pork chop; 2. the rib, e.g. *costata di manzo* = rib-eye steak.

costarelle [koh-sta-**rell**-ay] spare ribs.

costoletta [kos-toh-**let**-ah] a cutlet or chop of pork, lamb or veal, also called *cotoletta*. *Costoletta milanese* is a thinly breaded veal chop, in effect a Wiener Schnitzel. *Costoletta a orecchia di elefante*, the 'elephant-ear cutlet', is a larger incarnation.

Schnitzel or *costoletta*?

Culinary historians disagree about the origins of the *costoletta milanese*, the famous dish of golden brown fried breaded veal. Some claim ancestry in Milan (hence *alla milanese*); others claim that it is Viennese (*Wiener Schnitzel*), perhaps via Constantinople. Austria and Northern Italy have not lacked historical links, and it is highly likely that it was introduced from one to the other. During the Habsburg occupation of Lombardy, Milan was home to a large Austrian garrison, and it has been suggested that Field Marshal Radetzky (for whom Strauss wrote the *Radetzky March*) so loved the dish that he took the recipe back with him to Austria.

---

cotechino [kot-ay-**keen**-oh] a large, spiced pork sausage.

cotogna [kot-**on**-ya] quince.

cotoletta [kot-oh-**let**-ah] a chop, see COSTOLETTA.

cotto/a [**kot**-oh] cooked.

cotturo [koh-**toor**-oh] copper cauldron (Abruzzo); *al cotturo* describes a dish cooked in such a cauldron, typically a stew.

couscous [**koos**-koos] a

durum wheat staple popular throughout southern Italy, one of the contributions of the North African Maghreb to Italian cuisine. Some of the traditional dishes that use couscous are strikingly reminiscent of the Maghrebi tradition that uses spiced lamb and vegetables. There is an annual couscous fair in Sicily around Sept. The *cuscussu* of Tuscan Jewish cuisine, served with meatballs on the feast of *Tu B'Shvat* (the 'New Year of the Trees', Feb) was probably the import of Spanish Jews who fled to Livorno in the 16th century to avoid persecution. See also FREGULA.

coviglia [koh-**vee**-lyah] a mousse (Naples), usually coffee or chocolate-flavoured.

cozza [**kot**-sah] mussel (pl. *cozze*).

crafi see KRAFI.

crauti [**krow**-tee] sauerkraut, common in the north, especially in Trentino-Alto Adige.

crema [**kray**-mah] 1. a creamy sauce or purée. *Crema*

Cozza, a mussel shell.

di legumi is creamed vegetables or vegetable cream soup; 2. custard pudding made with eggs and milk. *Crema frangipane* is custard made with egg yolks, milk, crushed almonds and vanilla; *crema inglese* is custard made with egg yolks and milk, omitting flour; *crema pasticcera* is confectioner's custard, thickened with flour and eggs.

cremoso/a [kray-**moh**-zoh] creamy or thick.

cren [kren] in the northern regions, horseradish.

crescentina, crescenta [kray-shen-**teen**-ah, kray-**shen**-tah] a flatbread that puffs up when fried into small pillows of dough. The name comes from the Latin *crescere*, to grow. In and around Modena a similar flatbread is baked between *tigelle* [tee-**jel**-ay], traditional stone moulds.

crescenza [kray-**shent**-sah] a soft, creamy, fresh cow's milk cheese, also known as *stracchino*, typical of Lombardy, though it is also made elsewhere.

crescia [**kray**-sha] a type of soft bread, typical of the Marche, studded with pieces of cheese and/or SALUME.

crescia al testo [**kray**-sha al **tay**-stoh] a circular bread of pizza-type dough from the Gubbio area of Umbria, sliced in half and eaten with a variety of fillings. Also known as *torta al testo*.

cresc' tajat [kraysh tie-**at**] originally a peasant dish, a way of using up leftover polenta that had stuck to the sides of the pot. Added to flour and water to make pasta, and traditionally served with *sugo finto*, 'mock sauce', little cuts of GUANCIALE and diced vegetables.

crescione [kray-**show**-nay] cress.

crespelle [kray-**spell**-ay] crêpes, pancakes.

creste di galli [**kray**-stay dee **gall**-ee] cocks' combs; also a short-cut pasta suitable for salads or soups.

crispelle, crispelli see CRE-SPELLE.

crispigno [kree-**speen**-yoh] sow thistle, a wild herb similar in appearance to a dandelion, said by Pliny the Elder to have been eaten by Theseus prior to his battle with the Bull of Marathon.

croccante [kroh-**kan**-teh] (pl. *croccanti*) crispy, e.g. *crosta croccante*: a crispy crust.

crocchette [kro-**kett**-ay] croquettes. *Croquette di pesce* [dee **pay**-shay] are fishcakes.

crosta [**kross**-tah] crust, e.g. of a pie.

crostata [kross-**tah**-tah] (pl. *crostate*) a pie or tart, either sweet or savoury, e.g. *crostata di frutta*, a fruit tart.

crostini [kross-**tee**-nee] miniature slices of bread, toasted and spread with a variety of toppings, e.g. anchovies, tomatoes etc, often served as bite-sized canapés; see also CROSTONI.

crostoli [**kross**-toh-lee] pastry strips or ribbons fried and sprinkled with powdered sugar.

crostoni [kross-**toh**-nee] large CROSTINI, sometimes sufficient to bear an entire pork chop, in effect, 'rustic' canapés.

crudo 1. raw, rare; 2. cured, in the case of SALUME, fish or ham.

crumiri [kroo-**mee**-ree] half-moon-shaped biscuits from Piedmont.

crusca di frumento [kroos-kah dee froo-**main**-toh] bran.

cubbaita [koo-**bite**-ah] Sicilian nougat of Arab origin.

cubetti [koo-**bet**-ee] cubes, *cubetti di ghiaccio* [**gyah**-choh], ice cubes.

cuccìa [koo-**chee**-ah] a dessert of boiled grains of wheat and RICOTTA sweetened with candied fruit, eaten in Palermo on 13th Dec, the feast of Santa Lucia, in commemora-

tion of the saint's deliverance of the city from famine in 1646.

cucina [koo-**chee**-nah] kitchen, cuisine, style of cooking.

cucina povera [koo-**chee**-nah **poh**-vay-rah] so-called 'poor' cuisine, the fashionable reincarnation of low-budget rustic staples as venerable regional dishes. Though the phenomenon has its pretensions, it has done much to stimulate international interest in regional Italian cooking.

cuddhurite [koo-dhoo-**reet**-ay] ring-shaped PASTINA from Sicily.

culaccio [koo-**latch**-oh] rump.

culatello [koo-lah-**tell**-oh] a cured ham made with pork rump; the best *culatello* (it has DOP status) is said to be found in the Zibello region of the Parma lowlands, Emilia-Romagna.

culingionis [kool-een-**joan**-ees] Sardinian PASTA RIPIENA resembling mini pasties, typically stuffed with potatoes,

PECORINO and mint or other greens. Also known as *culurzones*, *kulurjones* or *culurjones*.

culurgiones, culurzones see CULINGIONIS.

cumino [koo-**mee**-noh] cumin; *cumino tedesco* is caraway.

cuoco [**kwoh**-koh] cook, chef.

cuore [**kwoh**-ray] the heart, e.g. of an artichoke, as opposed to its *fondo* (base). *Cuori di sedano* [**kwoh**-ree dee **say**-dan-oh] are celery hearts.

curcuci bacon rind, pork crackling.

cusco see CUSCUS

cuscus see COUS COUS.

cutanei [koot-an-**ay**-ee] GNOC-CHI from the Marche, served with a meat RAGÙ.

cuzzetielle [koot-say-tee-**ell**-ay] type of pasta from Molise, hollowed in the centre or curled like CAVATELLI, traditionally served with meat (particularly hare) RAGÙ.

cuzzi [**koot**-see] irregular pasta shapes, 'cuts', popular in Lazio. As with many staples once humble peasant fare, *cuzzi* now have a niche following; there is a festival in their honour held every July in Roviano.

cuzzupe [koot-**zoop**-ay] sweet Easter breads from Calabria, made in a variety of shapes.

Cynar [chee-**nar**] a popular bitter liqueur, drunk either as an APERITIVO or DIGESTIVO, made with artichokes and a variety of herbs.

dadi [**dah**-dee] cubes.

dalle and **alle** with opening times, from and to: e.g. *dalle ore 9:30 alle 14:30*: from 9.30am to 2.30pm.

datteri [**dah**-tay-ree] dates.

datteri di mare [**dah**-tay-ree dee **mah**-ray] 'sea dates', large shellfish once considered a great delicacy. They burrow into rocks, making tunnels for themselves to live in, with the result that fishing them required destruction of marine habitats. It has now been outlawed in most EU states.

decaffeinato [day-kaff-ay-ee-**nah**-toh] decaffeinated.

degli see DEL.

degustazione [day-goo-stats-ee-**own**-ay] tasting, e.g. a 'tasting menu', where a number of dishes in a restaurant's repertoire are offered for a set price.

del, dello, della, delle, degli of, any, some e.g. *delle acciughe*: some anchovies; *del bosco*: of (from) the forest.

dente, al [**dayn**-tay] firm (of pasta). The opposite of *al dente* is *stracotto*: soggy.

dentice [**dayn**-tee-chee] dentex (fish).

denti di cavallo [**dayn**-tee dee kah-**val**-oh] 'horse's teeth', a short, narrow pasta tube. Also known as *denti di pecora* ('sheep's teeth').

denti di leone [**dayn**-tee dee lay-**own**-ay] dandelions.

denti di pecora [**dayn**-tee dee **payk**-or-ah] see DENTI DI CAVALLO.

diavoletti [dee-ah-voh-**let**-ee] 'little devils', pasta in the form of slim curved tubes.

diavolicchio [dee-ah-voh-**lee**-kee-oh] chilli (Abruzzo).

diavolillo [dee-ah-voh-**leel**-oh] the 'little devil', an intensely hot chilli (*peperoncino rosso*) from Abruzzo and Molise.

digestivo [dee-jess-**tee**-voh] an alcoholic drink thought to have health-giving properties and to aid the digestion if taken after meals. A number of *digestivi* are found throughout Italy, many of them herbal infusions.

dindo, dindio [**deen**-doh, **deen**-dee-oh] a dialect word for turkey (*tacchino*).

dischi [**dees**-kee] discs, circular pasta shapes; variants include MESSICANI and *dischi volanti* [**dees**-kee voh-**lan**-tee], 'flying saucers'.

distillati [dee-stee-**lah**-tee] spirits, e.g. gin, vodka, whisky, brandy, GRAPPA.

dita degli apostoli [**dee**-tah day-lee ah-**poh**-stoh-lee] 'Apostles', fingers': miniature pancakes filled with RICOTTA flavoured with chocolate or citrus zest.

ditali [**dee**-tah-lee] small pasta 'thimbles' (also *ditalini* or *ditaletti*). Suitable for soups.

DOC/DOCG see VINO.

dolce [**dol**-chay] 1. sweet (adjective); 2. a sweet or dessert course (singular noun; pl. *dolci*).

dolcelatte [dol-chay-**lah**-tay] a smooth blue cheese, strong but milder than GORGONZOLA.

Dolcetto [dol-**chay**-toh] red-wine grape of Piedmont producing dark-coloured but lighter-drinking wines than the signature BAROLO.

dolci [**doll**-chee] desserts.

dolciume [dol-**choo**-may] sweets, candy, confectionery.

donderet [**don**-der-et] GNOCCHI from Piedmont served with butter and cheese.

donzelline [dont-sell-**een**-ay] deep-fried pasta, a Tuscan recipe (sweet and savoury versions exist), traditionally eaten at the Thrush Festival in the last week of Oct, which celebrates the hunting season for migratory birds.

DOP (*Denominazione di Origine Protetta*), the equivalent of an *appellation controlée* for food products, particularly cheese such as PARMIGIANO REGGIANO.

doppio/a [**doh**-pee-oh] double.

dragoncello [drag-on-**chell**-oh] tarragon.

duccara [doo-**kah**-rah] a wild Sicilian fig.

durke [**door**-kay] sweet (Sardinian).

duro/a [**doo**-roh] hard.

durone [doo-**roh**-nay] cherry.

e, ed and.

ecco! [**eck**-oh] behold! here it is! often said by waiters with impressive theatricality upon the presentation of even the most modest dish.

edule [**ay**-doo-lay] cockles.

eliche [**ell**-ee-kay] 'propellers', a pasta shape.

elicoidali [ell-ee-**coy**-dal-ee] spiral pasta shapes.

Emilia-Romagna [em-**ee**-lee-ah roh-**man**-yah] a region of central Italy dominated by the Po valley and delta. The principal cities are (on the seaboard) Ravenna and Rimini, and inland, Ferrara, Parma, Reggio, Piacenza and

Bologna. Specialities include egg pasta, such as TAGLIATELLE, and balsamic vinegar (see ACETO), PARMA ham, PARMESAN cheese and BOLOGNESE sauce.

enoteca [en-oh-**teck**-ah] a wine shop.

eperlano [ay-pair-**lah**-noh] smelt (fish).

equino/a [ay-**kwee**-noh] as in *carne equina*: horsemeat.

erba [**air**-bah] a herb (pl. *erbe*).

erba cipollina [**air**-bah chee-poh-**lee**-nah] chives.

erba San Pietro see FINOC-CHIO MARINO.

erbaggi [air-**badge**-ee] cooked vegetables.

erbazzone [air-bats-**own**-ay] a spinach and cheese pie from Emilia-Romagna. *Erbaz-zone dolce* is the sweetened version, a Jewish speciality.

erbe aromatiche [**air**-bay ah-roh-**mat**-ee-kay] aromatic herbs.

erbetella [air-bay-**tell**-ah] a handful of herbs.

espresso see CAFFÈ.

Est! Est!! Est!!! light white wine from Montefiascone, Lazio, usually a blend of MALVASIA and TREBBIANO. Its name comes from the story of a bishop's servant told to leave chalk messages on tavern doors where good wine was to be had ('est' being the Latin for 'is'; in other words, 'it's here!').

estivi [ess-**tee**-vee] summer dishes.

estragone [ess-tra-**goh**-nay] tarragon.

estratto [ess-**trat**-oh] extract.

etto [**eh**-to] Italian equivalent of the prefix hecto-, meaning 100. A price per *etto* is a price per 100g.

evo [**ay**-voh] as in *olio evo*, extra virgin olive oil.

fagiano, fagianello [fadge-**ahn**-oh, fadge-ahn-**ell**-oh] pheasant.

fagiano di monte [fadge-**ahn**-oh dee **moan**-tay] black grouse.

fagiolata [fadge-oh-**lah**-tah] bean soup.

fagioli [fah-**joh**-lee] haricot beans, brown or white, usually bought dried, soaked, and then stewed slowly. *Fagioli di pollo* are rooster testicles.

fagiolini [fadge-oh-**lee**-nee] French beans, long green beans.

fagiolini rigati [fadge-oh-**lee**-nee ree-**gah**-tee] pasta shapes, curved tubes approximately shaped like French beans.

fagiolone [fadge-oh-**loan**-ay] runner beans.

fainà [fay-ee-**nah**] Ligurian dialect for FARINATA.

fainelle [fie-ee-**nell**-ay] Puglian pasta, often cooked with potato and RUCOLA.

falloni [fall-**own**-ee] 'big phalluses', a pasta resembling a thin pancake, stuffed with vegetables.

faraona [farr-ah-**own**-ah] guinea fowl.

farcito/a [far-**chee**-toh] stuffed.

farfalle [far-**fall**-ay] pasta shaped like butterflies, good for salads.

farina [far-ee-nah] flour (*see box below*).

Types and grades of Italian flour

Flour for baking is usually obtained from *grano tenero* (*Triticum aestivum*). It is graded according to how refined it is; in other words, how much bran is left. '00' or *doppio zero*, the 'flower of flours' is a snow white powder with no bran at all. Other grades, less purely white because some bran remains, are '0', '1', '2' and '*integrale*' (wholemeal). For pasta-making, flour is obtained from durum wheat (*grano duro; Triticum durum*). This is a hard-grained variety which when milled reduces to a fine meal called semolina, which allows the cooked pasta to remain *al* DENTE. Not all Italian soil and terrain is suitable for wheat-growing, and in the past other flours, made of rye (*segale*), millet (*miglio*) and chickpeas (*ceci*) were widely used. They are still found today in traditional recipes.

farina gialla [**jall**-ah] 'yellow flour', a name for polenta, as in the recipe *zuppa di cavolo nero e farina gialla* (cabbage and cornmeal soup).

farinata [fah-ree-**nah**-tah] thick pancake somewhat resembling a Mexican *tortilla*, usually made of chickpea flour.

farinata di zucca [fah-ree-**nah**-tah di **tsoo**-kah] a Ligurian pie made of pumpkin and cheese.

farro [**fah**-roh] emmer wheat, an ancient, hard-grained variety. Thoroughly soaked before cooking, it is often used in soups and salads and is common in Tuscan cuisine.

fasui see FAGIOLI.

fasul, fasule [fa-**zool**, fa-**zool**-ay] dialect form of FAGIOLI.

fattisù [fat-ee-**soo**] a stuffed pasta from Emilia-Romagna typically with a filling of cabbage (*fattisù di verza*); the resulting parcel is 'done' or sealed (*fatti*) up (*sù*).

fava [**fah**-vah] broad beans, eaten fresh in spring and

Farfalle, 'butterfly pasta'.

early summer when small and tender; popular around Rome. *Favata* is a bean stew; *fave dei morti*, literally, 'beans of the dead', are little biscuits given to children on 2nd Nov, the Day of the Dead.

favata [fah-**vah**-tah] see FAVA.

fazzoletti [fatso-**lett**-ee] 'handkerchiefs', pasta sheets folded around a filling or topped with sauce.

fecata [**feck**-ah-tah] liver (Naples).

fecola [**feck**-oh-lah] starch, such as corn starch, used for thickening and baking.

fedde del cancelliere [fed-ay dell kan-chell-ee-**air**-ay] 'chancellor's buttocks', a Sicilian dessert made of semolina and pistachios or almonds, formed into a patty and served split down the middle so as to resemble the prosperous buttocks of a senior civil servant.

fegatazzo di Ortona [fay-gat-**at**-so dee or-**toh**-nah] a liver sausage from the Abruzzo.

fegatelli [fay-gat-**ell**-ee] diced pig's liver wrapped in strands of OMENTO; faggots.

fegatini [fay-gat-**ee**-nee] chicken livers.

fegatino [fay-gat-**ee**-noh] liver sausage from the Marche.

fegato [**fay**-gat-oh] liver.

Fernet Branca [fer-**net** bran-kah] a bitter DIGESTIVO made of roots and spices macerated in alcohol. It is manufactured in the Branca family distillery in Milan. The name Fernet is a combination of the French *fer* ('iron') and *net* ('clean'), a reference to the traditional process of stirring the liquor with a red-hot iron rod. Its supposed curative properties (in the early 20th century it was marketed as an effective safeguard against cholera) hark back to medieval times when monasteries and mountebanks would market herbal tonics and potions.

ferrazzuoli [fer-at-**swoh**-lee] long, thin pasta ribbons, slightly twisting, an effective way of trapping the sauce.

fesa [**fay**-zah] for beef and veal, the rump; for turkey, the breast.

fett'unta [fet-**oon**-tah] in Tuscany, dry bread rubbed with olive oil and garlic, also known as *panunta*.

fetta [**fet**-ah] a slice, e.g. *una fetta di pane*: a slice of bread (pl. *fette*).

fettina [fet-**een**-ah] a thin slice; *fettine di vitello* are veal escalopes.

fettucce, fettuccelle [fet-**ooh**-chay, fet-ooh-**chell**-ay] 'ribbons', a pasta shape.

fettuccine [fay-too-**chee**-nay] 'little ribbons', a long, flat egg-and-flour pasta similar to TAGLIATELLE.

fiadi [fee-**ahd**-ee] a type of ribbon pasta.

Fiano [fee-**ahn**-oh] ancient white-wine grape from Campania, used to produce the excellent Fiano di Avellino.

fiasco [fee-**ass**-koh] a flask. The Tuscan FAGIOLI (or CANNELLINI) *al fiasco* are beans stewed over charcoal with garlic and sage in a traditional straw-protected flask.

ficatu [fee-kah-too] liver (Sicily).

fico [fee-koh] (pl. *fichi*) fig. Warning: make sure you get the gender right. The feminine form, *fica*, is a slang word for female genitalia.

fideg, fidic Lombard and Piedmontese forms of *fegato*, liver.

fidelini [fee-day-**lee**-nee] very thin pasta strands.

fieno di canepina [fee-**ay**-noh dee can-ay-**pee**-nah] 'hay from Canepina', long pasta noodles, a speciality of Viterbo in Lazio, traditionally served with a sauce of chicken giblets.

figà [fee-**gah**] liver (Venice).

filateddi [feel-a-**tedh**-ee] a long ribbon-like pasta, a Sicil- ian variant of FETTUCCE.

filato/a [fee-**lah**-tee] 'spun'. *Zucchero filato* is spun sugar. *Formaggio a pasta filata* is a cheese such as MOZZARELLA, SCAMORZA or PROVOLONE, where the curds have been stretched and kneaded to an elastic consistency.

fileja [fee-**lay**-ya] rolled pasta from Calabria.

filetto [fee-**lay**-toh] fillet (UK), tenderloin (US).

filindeu [fee-leen-**day**-oo] the 'threads of God'. Very thin sheet of pasta resembling a rush mat or piece of gauze, traditionally 'woven' by hand. It is a speciality of Nuoro in Sardinia, where it is used in soups.

filone [fee-**loan**-ay] 1. an elongated bread roll, a short baguette; 2. see SCHIENALE.

finferli see CANTARELLI.

finanziera [fee-nan-tsee-**ay**-rah] a Piedmontese stir-fry of cocks' combs and veal sweetbreads with mushrooms and MARSALA.

fino/a [**fee**-no] fine.

finocchio [fee-**nock**-ee-oh]
fennel. The bulbous base of
the stem is a popular vegetable. The feathery leaves are
used as a herb and the dried
seeds are a valuable spice.

finocchio marino [fee-**nock**-
ee-oh mah-**ree**-noh] rock
samphire (*Crithmum mar-
itimum*), a shrub that grows
on cliffs and seashores. Its
aromatic leaves are eaten raw
or pickled. Also known as
erba di San Pietro or *critamo*.

finocchiona [fee-nock-ee-
own-ah] Tuscan SALAME
flavoured with fennel seeds.

fiocchetti see CHIACCHIERE.

fiocchi d'avena [fee-**ock**-ee
dah **vay**-nah] oat flakes.

fiocchi di mais [fee-**ock**-ee
dee **mice**] cornflakes.

fior di latte [**fyor** dee lah-tay]
a MOZZARELLA made from
cow's, not buffalo's, milk. See
also GELATO.

fiore sardo [fee-**or**-ay **sar**-
doh] hard Sardinian sheep's
milk cheese.

fiore di zucca [fee-**or**-ay dee
tsoo-kah] courgette/zucchini

flowers, stuffed with anchovy
and fried in light batter.

fiorone [fee-or-**own**-ay] fig
(pl. *fioroni*).

fischiotti, fischioni [fees-
kee-**ott**-ee, fees-kee-**own**-ee]
tubular pasta from Abruzzo.

fisckariedd' [fee-ska-ree-**ed**]
irregularly-shaped offcuts left
over from RAVIOLI-making,
served in soup, originating in
the poorer areas of Basilicata.

fiyat [**fee**-at] liver (Friuli).

focaccia [foh-**catch**-ah]
savoury flatbread baked in
a variety of ways: *alla salvia*:
with sage; *alle olive*: with
olives; *alle noci*: with walnuts;
al rosmarino: with rosemary.
Focaccia ripiena is *focaccia*
filled before baking, typically
with MOZZARELLA and ham.
The word originates from the
Latin *panis focacius*, 'bread
from the hearth' (*focus* in
Latin means hearth, the 'focal'
point of the home).

foglia [**foe**-lee-ah] a leaf (pl.
foglie).

fojade [foe-**jah**-day] wide
noodles from Lombardy.

folletti [foll-**ett**-ee] elves, a
pasta shape.

fondo [**fon**-doh] base, bed.

fonduta [fon-**doo**-tah] 1. a
fondue, a mixture of melted
cheese and wine, sometimes
with truffles, into which
bread or vegetables may be
dipped, typical of the alpine
regions; 2. any 'melted' dish,
e.g. *fonduta di cioccolate*.

fontina [fon-**teen**-ah] a cow's
milk cheese from the Valle
d'Aosta.

formagella [fore-mah-**jel**-ah]
a delicate cow's milk cheese.

formaggio [fore-**madge**-oh]
cheese. In Italy it is made
from the milk of goats,
sheep, cows and, in the case
of MOZZARELLA, buffalo. The
taste and texture depends on
several factors, including the
plants on which the animals
graze, which contribute to the
flavour of the milk. *Formaggio a pasta dura* [**pas**-tah
doo-rah] is firm-textured
cheese; *formaggio a pasta molle*
[**moll**-ay] is soft. There are
many different types and con-

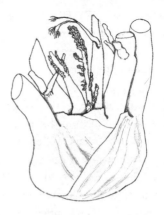

Fennel (*finocchio*). The plant's stem,
leaves and seeds are all edible.

sistencies of cheese in Italy.
Formaggi freschi are young,
fresh, delicate-tasting cheeses
such as MOZZARELLA and MAS-
CARPONE. *Formaggi duri* and
semiduri are made by taking
smaller portions of the coagulated whey and compressing
it to varying degrees. PROVO-
LONE is a *semiduro*, PECORINO
and PARMIGIANO are *duro*.
Many cheeses go through a
number of mutations in their
life cycle. There might be a
young, fresh version and a
harder, aged version of the
same cheese.

Formaggio di fossa

Literally 'pit-cheese', this is a strong cheese originating in Emilia-Romagna. At the end of summer the circular cheeses are wrapped in cloth and left in deep, circular pits or ditches hewn out of tufa, the volcanic rock of the area. Quantities of straw are burnt in the ditches to dry them out before they are lined with chalk. When the cheeses are stacked in place, the ditch is firmly sealed until 25th Nov, St Catherine's Day, when a mini festival is held to celebrate the new batch of *formaggio*. The tradition has its roots in a medieval scheme for evading papal tax. Well in advance of the tax agent's visit, the citizens of Sogliano al Rubicone would conceal their valuables—wine and imperishable food as well as cash—in the inner recesses of volcanic caves or in specially dug pits or ditches (*fosse*). Over time it became clear that these hiding places provided excellent refrigeration and that their internal humidity could be manipulated by careful sealing, lining and part-ventilation. Similar evasive measures were taken in the Veneto, where peasants hid their cheese in barrels of grape must. This was found to hasten the ripening process and increase longevity, and thus *formaio embriago* (*see below*) was born.

formai de mut [for-**my** deh **moot**] a tangy cow's milk cheese from the Alta Val Brembana near Bergamo, Lombardy.

formaio embriago [for-**my**-oh em-bree-**ah**-goh] literally 'drunken' cheese, originating in Treviso (Veneto), so called after the practice of immersing a cheese in red wine or grape must.

forno [for-no] oven, bakery; *forno a legna*: wood burning-oven; *al forno*: baked.

fragola [**frah**-go-lah] (pl.

fragole) 1. strawberry; *fragola di bosco* or *fragola selvatica*: wild strawberry; 2. *uva fragola*, the Concord grape.

fragolino [frah-go-**lee**-noh] 1. sea bream; 2. still or sparkling red wine from north Italy, made from FRAGOLA grapes.

Franciacorta [fran-cha-**kor**-tah] the premier Lombard DOCG, known for its white Chardonnay and red PINOT NERO, as well as for sparkling wines.

frantoiana [fran-toy-**ahn**-ah] e.g. *zuppa frantoiana*: a soup into which olive oil has been drizzled; from FRANTOIO.

frantoio [fran-**toy**-oh] the mill or press where olive oil is manufactured, often a family-run operation tucked away in the hills. Finer olive oil is often referred to as *olio di frantoio* to distinguish it from mass-produced oil.

frasca [**fras**-kah] in Friuli, a traditional tavern run by wine producers as a showcase for the latest vintage, also serving food to go with it. *Frasca* means a branch or twig. To show that the tavern was open, a branch was stuck up outside. The same tradition survives today in the *Buschen-schänke* of Austria.

frascarelli [fras-kah-**rell**-ee] irregularly-shaped lumps of pasta. The dough is traditionally moistened by flicking it with water from a small switch (*'frasca'*). *Frascarelli* are also known as *'nsaccaragatti*, 'cats in the bag'.

Frascati [fra-**skah**-tee] light white wine from the Alban Hills, south of Rome.

frascatielle [fras-kah-tee-**ell**-ay] see FRASCARELLI.

frattaglie [fratt-**ah**-lyay] offal.

fregnacce [frayn-**yatch**-ay] pasta triangles from Lazio, Abruzzo and the Marche, served in piquant, meaty sauces.

fregula, fregola [**fray**-goo-lah] Italian couscous, orginating in Sardinia. The semolina spheres are larger, about 2–3mm in diameter.

Freisa [**fray**-za] red-wine

Fusilli ('little spindles'), one of the most familiar of Italian pasta shapes.

grape from Piedmont that produces DOC-quality red and rosé wines, both 100 percent varietal and in blends.

fresco/a [**fray**-skoh] fresh, cool.

fricassea [free-cass-**ay**-ah] fricassée.

frico [free-koh] fried potato pancake from Friuli, with an outer layer of cheese.

frico balacia [**free**-koh bal-**ah**-chah] a cheese with a high melting point, ideal for grilling or frying (Friuli-Venezia Giulia). Also known as *balacin*.

frigulozzi [free-goo-**lot**-see] lengths of leavened bread dough boiled and served with tomato sauce and PECORINO. A speciality of Lazio.

friselle or **frisedde** [free-**zell**-ay, free-**zed**-ay] bread rings half-baked, cut in half and baked again (Puglia).

frittata [free-**tah**-tah] an omelette that has been turned over as opposed to folded in half. Compare OMELETTE.

fritto/a [**free**-toh] fried; *fritto misto* = a mixed fry-up; *fritto misto alla fiorentina* = a Florentine fry-up of meat, vegetables and offal; *fritto misto alla milanese* = a Milanese fry-up of brains, sweetbreads and courgettes.

frittole [**free**-toh-lay] doughnuts with candied fruit (Veneto).

Friuli-Venezia Giulia northeastern region of Italy reaching deep into Central Europe. The cuisine shows strong Austrian and Central European influence. There is a rich variety of cheese, soups and SALUMI: *Prosciutto di Dan Daniele* is famous. The staples are POLENTA and rice. The region also produces good fish, and some interesting wines, including Picolit.

frizzante [frid-**zant**-ay] of wine or water, sparkling.

frocia [**frotch**-ya] (Sicily) an omelette with RICOTTA and mint or peas.

frolla see PASTA FROLLA.

fromadzo [from-**adz**-oh] DOP cow's milk cheese from Valle d'Aosta.

froscia see FROCIA.

frullato [froo-**lah**-toh] a milkshake or smoothie.

frumento [froo-**mayn**-toh] wheat.

frumentone [froo-mayn-**toh**-nay] sweetcorn, maize.

frustega [froo-**stay**-gah] a pastry from the Marche cooked with grape must.

frustenga [froo-**stain**-gah] a cornmeal fruitcake.

frutta [**froo**-tah] fruit.

frutti [**froo**-tee] *frutti di mare* ('fruit of the sea') = seafood; *frutti di bosco* = 'fruit of the forest', i.e. mixed berries.

funchetti [foon-**ket**-ee] 'little mushroom', a PASTINA.

funghetto, al [al foon-**get**-oh] 'mushroom style', sliced and cooked as you would a mushroom.

funghi [**foon**-gee] mushrooms, hugely popular in Italy and widely available fresh in season or dried (*see box overleaf*).

furn [foorn] = FORNO.

fusi istriani [**foo**-zee ees-tree-**ahn**-ee] 'Istrian spindles' pasta from Friuli-Venezia Giulia and Istria, often served with a filling RAGÙ of chicken or game.

fusiddi [foos-**eedh**-ee] southern dialect for FUSILLI.

fusilli [foos-**eel**-ee] corkscrew-shaped pasta; *fusilli bucati* are *fusilli* with holes running down the middle; *fusilli stretti* are tightly wound *fusilli*; *fusilloni* are larger. Before machine production took over, the shapes were made by laboriously winding strips of dough around thin reed wands.

fusto [**foos**-toh] barrel, often of oak, used for ageing wine.

Gaglioppo [gall-**yop**-oh] grape variety imported to Calabria from Greece, the main constituent of red Cirò.

Italian mushroom mania

Principal varieties of Italian mushroom include *colombina* (Columbine), *colombina dorata* (golden Columbine), *chiodino* (the honey mushroom), *prataiolo* (the meadow mushroom), *lattario delizioso* (the milk cap), *spugnola* (the morel), the *porcino* (perhaps the best-known outside Italy) and the *vescia* (the puffball). A *trun* [troon], meaning 'thunder' in Piedmontese dialect, is a plump, apricot-coloured mushroom; a *gallinaccio* [gah-lee-**natch**-oh] is a chanterelle; *famiglioli* [fam-eel-**yo**-lee] are red, flat-topped mushrooms with yellow rays on the underside of the cap; the ruffled fungus known as *grifola* [**gree**-foh-lah] requires prolonged boiling and baking to make it edible.

Funghi secchi [**seck**-ee] are dried mushrooms. Edible funghi are known as *funghi buoni*, 'good mushrooms'. Poisonous funghi are *funghi velenosi*, the deadliest of which are known as *funghi mortali*: consumption of these is almost certain to be fatal. Novice mushroom gatherers should beware. The edible *ovolo buono*, for example, looks very like its poisonous cousin the *ovolo malefico*, also known as Satan's boletus. One of the most fearful of the *funghi velenosi*, it resembles the typical storybook mushroom, red-capped and plump-stemmed, the seat of fairies and pixies. When eaten, it provokes infernal hallucinations and agonising muscular spasms. A *fungaiolo* [foon-guy-**oh**-loh] is a mushroom hunter. There is a significant mortality rate among intrepid *fungaioli*, occasioned not by poisonous mushrooms but by climbing accidents. The rarer species grow in out-of-the-way places and many a *fungaiolo* has been found at the bottom of a deep crevasse, limbs broken but heroically clutching the prize.

galani [gall-**ah**-nee] fried pastries from northeast Italy.

galantina [gall-an-**tee**-nah] galantine, cold meat stuffed with forcemeat.

galba [**gal**-bah] in Milan and Lombardy, a popular name for a hearty vegetable soup.

galletto [gall-**ett**-oh] a pullet, in other words a young hen, under a year old.

gallina [gall-**ee**-nah] a hen (older than a POLLO), a stewing fowl, an old broiler.

gallinacci see CANTARELLI.

gallinella [gall-ee-**nell**-ah] 1. gurnard (fish); 2. see POLLANCA.

gallo [**gal**-oh] a cock, rooster.

gallo cedrone [**gal**-oh ched-**roh**-nay] grouse, literally the 'cedar cock', from its habitat.

gallo forcello [**gall**-oh for-**chay**-loh] black grouse.

Gallo Nero [**gall**-oh **nay**-roh] 'black cockerel'. The emblem of the black rooster on a yellow background is used as a mark of quality and authenticity by producers of CHIANTI CLASSICO.

gallurese [gall-oo-**ray**-zay] 'Gallura style', named after an area of northern Sardinia.

gamberelli [gam-bay-**rell**-ee] small prawns.

gamberetti [gam-bay-**ret**-ee] shrimps.

gamberi [**gam**-bay-ree] prawns.

gamberi di fiume [**gam**-bay-roh dee fee-**oo**-may] also *gamberi d'acqua dolce*, crayfish.

gambero imperiale [gam-bay-roh eem-pay-ree-**ah**-lay] large prawn.

Gambero Rosso [**gam**-bay-roh **ross**-oh] influential food and wine publishing group. Its guides and listings are a good source of information on gastronomic developments in Italy. The name means 'The Red Prawn', after the inn in the Pinocchio story.

garbanzo [gar-**bants**-oh] chickpea.

Garganega [gar-gan-**ay**-ga] white grape from the Veneto, used to produce SOAVE.

garganelli [gar-gan-**ell**-ee] ridged pasta squares curled over on themselves into a tube shape, resembling a gullet or *garganel*.

gargati [gar-**gah**-tee] PASTA CORTA from the Veneto, served with a meat sauce.

garofalato [gar-oh-fal-**ah**-toh] beef or lamb cooked in red wine and cloves.

garofano [gar-oh-**fah**-noh] *chiodi di garofano* are cloves.

garusolo SEE MURICE.

gassata [gass-**ah**-tah] carbonated.

gasse [**gass**-ay] bow-shaped PASTINA from Liguria.

gattafin [gatt-ah-**feen**] deep-fried pasta parcels from Liguria, filled with herbs, eggs and cheese.

Gattinara [gah-tee-**nah**-rah] long-lived red wine from Piedmont, made mainly from NEBBIOLO, in good years capable of rivalling a BAROLO.

gattò [gat-**oh**] a Neapolitan potato pie with ham and cheese.

gattuccio [gah-**too**-choh] dogfish.

gè in preixun [jay een prake-**soon**] 'chard in prison', Genoese slang for PANSOTTI.

gelatina [jell-ah-**teen**-ah] gelatin, jelly, aspic.

gelato [jell-**ah**-toh] ice cream.

Italian *gelato*

In AD 62 the emperor Nero, with characteristic panache, ordered relays of slaves along the Appian Way to ferry buckets of ice and snow from the Apennine mountain ranges to Rome. This, mixed with honey and berries, was the forerunner of modern ice cream and made a kind of sorbet similar in texture to those that had been popular in the Mediterranean since the 5th century BC, when the Greek physician Hippocrates had promoted the health-giving properties of ice to his patients. Throughout the Arab world sorbets of a similar kind developed along parallel lines. In Baghdad under the Abbasid caliphs,

great improvements were made to sorbets by the addition of cream. The fertile exchange of ideas among Jewish, Arabic and Christian scholars throughout the Middle Ages brought about dramatic changes in gastronomy as well as in mainstream science and art. To the great benefit of gastronomy, the aggressive expansionism of the Crusades stimulated rather than inhibited that exchange of ideas, all of which helped bring the ancient sorbet closer in form to the ice cream we enjoy today. The Arab occupation of Sicily, followed by the intermingling of Arab and Christian culture under Norman rule, had a profound influence on all southern Italian dishes including the sorbet. The Renaissance saw innovations by Bernardo Buontalenti (1536–1608), a Florentine engineer in the service of the Medici and a notable pioneer of refrigeration. In the Baroque era there were further developments set in motion by Francesco Procopio dei Coltelli (fl.1650–1720), a Sicilian restaurateur who developed an early ice cream-making machine. Ice cream has its mythology too, central to which is the persistent myth that Marco Polo discovered both ice cream and pasta in China and brought them back to Europe.

Gelato today is served in a cup (*coppa*) or cone (*cono*) and comes in a variety of *gusti* (flavours). These include a variety of fruit flavours, many kinds of chocolate, coffee, spices and some others, including: *bacio* [**bah**-cho], 'a kiss', a chocolate hazelnut mix; *cioccolato all' azteca* [cho-koh-**lah**-toh al-az-**tay**-kah] with cinnamon and hot pepper; *fior di latte* [**fyor** dee **lah**-tay], sweet, creamy, milk ice cream; *gianduja* or *gianduia* [jan-**doo**-ya], chocolate and hazelnut; *malaga* [**mah**-lah-gah], rum and raisin; *riso* [**ree**-zoh], rice, somewhat like rice pudding; *puffo* [**poof**-foh], a sort of bubblegum flavour; *stracciatella* [strah-cha-**tel**-lah], chocolate chips in a *fior di latte* base; *Viagra*, a curiosity, not containing the drug itself but, instead, various herbs that are said to be used in Viagra and to have an aphrodisiac effect; *zabaione* [zah-bah-**yoh**-nay], a foundation of egg and custard with a MARSALA *leitmotif*.

Granita siciliana is a kind of crushed water ice; *semifreddi* are ice cream cakes.

gelone [jell-**own**-ay] oyster mushroom.

gelso [**jell**-soh] mulberry.

gemelli [jem-**ell**-ee] 'twins', two short pasta strands twisted together.

genepì [jen-e-**pee**] a liqueur from the Valle d'Aosta and Savoy region made from herbs of the wormwood family.

geretto [jeh-ray-toh] shank, the cut used for OSSO BUCO.

geriebenes Gerstl [guh-**ree**-ben-us **gair**-stl] a pasta GRAT-TUGIATA from northern Friuli.

germogli [jair-**moh**-lyee] sprouts, sprouted seeds.

ghiacciato/a [gee-atch-**ah**-toh] ice-cold, chilled.

ghiacciolo [**gyah**-choh-loh] an ice lolly, popsicle.

ghianda [gee-**and**-ah] acorn.

ghiotta, alla [gee-**ott**-ah] *pesce spada alla ghiotta* is swordfish cooked in a sauce of tomatoes, olives and capers.

ghiozzo [gee-**ot**-soh] goby, a small fish, eaten in RISOTTO.

gianduia, gianduiotto, gianduja [jan-**doo**-ya, jan-doo-**yot**-toh] a Piedmontese speciality, hazelnut and chocolate.

gigli [**jee**-lee] 'lilies', PASTINA slightly resembling a calla lily flower.

ginepro [jee-**nay**-pro] juniper, used in marinades and stews and to season ham.

Gingerino [jeen-jay-**ree**-noh] a ginger-flavoured aperitif.

gioddù [jo-**doo**] Sardinian yoghurt.

giorno [jor-noh] day, e.g.
specialità [spetch-ah-lee-**tah**]
del giorno: today's special.

giovane [joe-van-ay] young.

Giovedì Grasso [joe-vay-**dee**
grah-soh] Shrove Tuesday.

girello [jee-**ray**-loh] topside
or silverside of beef or pork,
suitable for stews.

giudea, giudia, alla [joo-**day**-
ah] in the Jewish style. In the
case of artichokes, this means
flattened and fried whole.

giuggiulena [joo-joo-**lay**-nah]
sesame snaps or sesame nou-
gat from Sicily.

giuncata, giuncà [joon-**kah**-
tah, joon-**kah**] an unsalted
fresh cheese.

gizzoa [gits-**oh**-ah] a flatbread
pouch ideal for meat or vegetable fillings (Liguria).

gloria patri [gloh-ree-ah
pah-tree] 'Glory be to the
Father', a ring-shaped PASTINA,
the name being an allusion
to the widespread practice of
reciting short prayers to time
cooking in the days before
people had clocks.

gnocchetti [nyock-**et**-ee] little

GNOCCHI.

gnocchi [**nyock**-ee] thick,
soft dumplings made from a
variety of ingredients, which
can include semolina, wheat
flour, potato and bread-
crumbs; a single example is a
gnocco; they may be eaten as a
starter or as the pasta course.
Traditionally they are served
with tomato sauces, pesto,
and in melted butter, with
sage (*see box opposite*).

Gnoccolar see VENERDÌ.

gnomirelli [no-mee-**rell**-ee]
faggots or sausages, usually of
lamb's offal.

gnudi [**noo**-dee] see *Some
types of gnocchi*, opposite.

gnumareddi [nu-mah-**redh**-
ee] see GNOMIRELLI.

gò [goh] see GHIOZZO.

gobeletti [goh-beh-**lay**-tee]
see COBELETTI.

gobbo [**goh**-boh] alternative
name for the cardoon (see
CARDI), from the Italian *gobbo*,
a dwarf.

gocce di cioccolato [gotch-
ay dee chock-oh-**lah**-toh]
chocolate chips.

Some types of *gnocchi*

Gnocchi can be round, ovoid, elongated or flat. They can be smooth or ridged. They are always cooked for a very short time, in boiling water, removed as soon as they float to the surface.

Gnocchi di zucca [**tsoo**-kah] are dumplings made with squash, typically served with butter and cheese. *Gnocchi ossolani* [oss-oh-**lah**-nee], from Piedmont, are made with chestnut flour, mashed potato and pumpkin purée. *Gnocchi ricci* [**ree**-chee], from Amatrice in northern Lazio, made with two doughs, one made of flour and eggs and the other of flour and water. The doughs are kneaded together, then pieces are broken off and dragged and pressed through flour to make the distinctive, flattened *gnocchi*.

The ***gnocco gigante*** is a giant dumpling; a potato *gnocco* from Parma weighing 58.5 kg entered the Guinness Book of Records in May 2010.

Gnudi are dumplings made of RICOTTA and flour, called *gnudi* ('naked') because they look like RAVIOLI filling without the ravioli coat.

goccio [**gotch**-oh] a drop.

gogotto [go-**got**-oh] leg of lamb.

Gorgonzola [gore-gon-**tsohl**-ah] a veined blue DOP cheese, of cow's or goat's milk, widely made in Piedmont and Lombardy. It is named from the town of Gorgonzola, now a suburb of Milan, which was an early centre of production. The penicillin spores that create the blue mould are added to the milk, and when the curds have coagulated, metal nails (formerly made of hardwood) are inserted to create ventilated channels in which the mould can grow (if you cut open a cheese, you can see the tracks of these very clearly). In the past, cheeses were left to mature in ice-pits in the hills. Today's refrigeration technology makes these obsolete, though some producers still cling to the old techniques, and use Brown Swiss cows instead of Holstein Friesians, whose milk yield is higher.

graffe [grah-fay] ring-shaped Neapolitan doughnuts, sprinkled with sugar.

gramigna [grah-**meen**-ya] short pasta curls.

grana [grah-nah] fine-grained cheese, e.g. PARMIGIANO REGGIANO (parmesan) and *Grana Padano*, both hard cheeses originating in the Po Valley in Emilia-Romagna. *Grana Padano* matures faster than *Parmigiano*, and there are fewer rules about what the cows may eat, making it a more economical option. Another *grana* cheese is *Granone lodigiano* [grah-**noh**-nay loh-

dee-**jah**-noh] from Lombardy.

granchio [**gran**-kee-oh] (pl. *granchi*) crab.

grandinine [gran-dee-**nee**-nay] 'little hailstones', a pasta shape.

granelli [grah-**nell**-ee] testicles.

granita [grah-**nee**-tah] an iced dessert, often quite chunky, like a Slush Puppie or snow cone, made by freezing a syrup of water, sugar and flavouring of fruit, coffee, almonds or chocolate.

grano arso [**grah**-no **are**-so] literally, 'scorched wheat' (in Puglian dialect *gren iars*). After threshing, arable fields were burnt in order to fertilise the ground. The *grano arso* was the grain that had escaped the attention of the gleaners and survived the fire. It was gathered up and made into flour by the needy. Today the smoky flavour that it imparted to traditional dishes is much sought-after, and grain is specially toasted to recreate the effect. *Grano arso* flour is also available.

grano duro [grah-no **doo**-roh] durum wheat (*Triticum durum*), a hard grain high in gluten, used for making pasta.

Granone lodigiano see GRANA.

grano saraceno [**grah**-no sah-rah-**chay**-no] buckwheat.

granoturco [gran-**tour**-koh] sweetcorn, maize.

granseola [gran-say-**oh**-lah] spider crab. They are common on menus in the northern Adriatic region.

granum paradisi [grah-noom pah-rah-**dee**-zee] 'grains of paradise', see AFRAMOMO.

grappa [grah-pah] a spirit steam-distilled from pomace, the pressed skins and seeds of grapes left over after wine-making. *Grappa* exists in many regional variants, and there is a broad spectrum of quality too. Many wineries simply deliver their pomace to a central distillery and receive *grappa* in return. Others follow traditional artisanal methods, producing *grappa* that is accorded the same status as single-malt whiskies are in Britain, the USA and Japan. There is much gimmickry—oddly-shaped bottles, exotic flavours—but there is, nevertheless, excellent *grappa* to be discovered throughout Italy, though its real home is the north, particularly Friuli. *Grappa* is drunk as a DIGESTIVO. The *bussùl* [boo-**sool**] is the traditional shot-glass used for quaffing it; the *quartino* [kwar-**tee**-noh] is the jug by which a measure of *grappa* was traditionally ordered.

grasso [grah-so] fat.

graticola, alla [alla grah-tee-

Granseola, the spider crab.

koh-lah] barbequed, grilled.

gratinato/a [grah-tee-**nah**-toh] *au gratin*, i.e. browned in the oven or under the grill with a topping made of breadcrumbs and/or cheese.

graton d'oca [grah-**ton** **doh**-kah] Piedmontese goose SALAME.

grattoni [grah-**tone**-ee] small pasta lozenges, good for soup.

grattugiato/a [grah-too-**jah**-toh] grated. *Grattugiata* is used to describe broken bits of pasta used in a soup.

graviuole [grah-vee-**wole**-ay] pasta from Molise, tradition-ally served with wild boar RAGÙ.

Grechetto [gray-**ket**-oh] white-wine grape grown in Umbria; blended with TREB-BIANO grapes to produce the pleasant, dry Orvieto wine.

Greco [gray-koh] southern Italian wine grape, possibly introduced from ancient Greece. Both white-and red-wine varieties exist, though the most celebrated are the white *Greco di Tufo* (a DOCG from Campania) and *Greco di Bianco* (a DOC dessert wine from Calabria).

gremolata, gremolada [gray-moh-**lah**-tah, gray-moh **lah**-dah] a seasoning of chopped herbs, lemon and garlic.

gren iars SEE GRANO ARSO.

grespino [gray-**spee**-noh] see CRISPIGNO.

gribiche [gree-**bee**-kay] mayonnaise with capers and tarragon.

grigette [gree-**jet**-ay] small snails.

griglia, alla [**gree**-lee-ah] grilled.

grigliata [gree-lee-**ah**-tah] grill or barbecue, e.g. *grigliata mista*: a mixed grill.

Grignolino [gree-nyoh-**lee**-noh] red-wine grape grown almost exclusively in the Piedmont region, producing young-drinking tannic wines.

Grillo [**gree**-loh] Sicilian white grape with a high sugar con-tent, one of the main compo-nents of MARSALA.

grispelle [gree-**spell**-ay] see CRESPELLE.

grissini [gree-**see**-nee] breadsticks, said to have been invented in 1679 by a Turin doctor for King Vittorio Amedeo II of Savoy, who had a weak digestion and could not tolerate ordinary bread.

grolla dell'amicizia [groh-lah dell am-ee-**cheet**-see-ah]literally, the 'grail of friendship', in the Valle d'Aosta and Piedmont, a wooden loving cup, shaped like a multi-spouted teapot for serving coffee laced with GRAPPA.

grongo [**gron**-goh] conger eel (pl. *gronghi*).

grostoli [**groh**-stoh-lee] type of fritters in Trentino-Alto Adige.

gruviera [groovy-**air**-ah] a mild cheese from Northern Italy, the name derived from Gruyère.

guancia, guanciola [gwan-chah, gwan-**choh**-la] of an animal or fish, the cheek.

guanciale [gwan-**chah**-lay] cured pig's cheek, thought by many to be the ideal ingredient for CARBONARA sauce.

guarnazione [gwahr-nats-**yoh**-nay] garnish.

guastedda, guastella see VASTEDDA.

guatto see GHIOZZO.

guelfi, gueffus [**gwel**-fee, **gwe**-foos] almond and orange blossom sweetmeats from Sardinia.

Hoch Pustertaler [hoch **poo**-stair-**tah**-ler] cow's milk cheese from South Tyrol (Trentino-Alto Adige), also known as *formaggio Alta Pusteria* [**al**-tah poo-stair-**ee**-ah].

ice cream see GELATO.

IGP *Indicazione Geografica Protetta*, a seal of quality awarded to products whose geographical source is considered to be vital to their character or quality. CASTELLUCCIO lentils, for example, are only certainly from Castelluccio if they say IGP on the packet.

IGT Similar to IGP. See VINO.

imbottigliato [ihm-boh-tee-lee-**ah**-toh] bottled. See VINO.

imbottito/a [eem-boh-**teet**-oh] stuffed, filled.

impanadas [eem-pan-**ah**-das]

PASTA RIPIENA from Sardinia in the form of substantial pockets with a variety of fillings such as meat and vegetables or eels and cheese. *Impanadas* are often deep fried but can also be oven baked.

impanato/a [eem-pan-**ah**-toh] breaded.

impanatiglie see 'MPANATIGGHI.

impepata [eem-peh-**pah**-ta] e.g *impepata di cozze*, see PEPATA.

incapriata [een-kah-pree-**ah**-tah] Puglian vegetable dish known locally as *'ncapriata* or *maccù*, a *purée* of FAVA beans served with sautéed chicory.

inchiostro di seppia [een-**kyoss**-troh dee **sep**-ee-ah] cuttlefish ink.

indivia [een-**dee**-vee-ah] endive or curly lettuce. *Indivia riccia* is frisée.

indugghia [een-**doo**-gee-ah] a Calabrese pork and offal sausage, known locally as *'ndugghia* or *nuglia*, similar to the French *andouille*.

infornato/a [een-for-**nah**-toh] baked.

infusioni [een-foo-zee-**oh**-nee] infusions, herbal teas.

insaccato [een-sack-**ah**-toh] a sausage, literally, the 'in the bag', because of the intestine it is stuffed into (pl. *insaccati*).

insalata [een-sah-**lah** tah] salad; *mista* (mixed); *verde* (green); *caprese* (with tomatoes, MOZZARELLA and basil).

insalatina [een-sah-lah-**tee**-nah] a little salad.

integrale [een-tay-**grah**-lay] wholemeal; *riso integrale* is brown rice.

intingolo [een-**teen**-goh-loh] a sauce or gravy.

intongolo see INTINGOLO.

inv. min. frequently used on menus of cheese, seasoned ham, vinegar, etc., an abbreviation for *invecchiato minimo*, 'aged for at least', e.g. *inv. min. 24 mesi* (aged for at least 24 months).

invecchiato [een-vay-kee-**ah**-toh] aged, matured.

invecchiato minimo see INV. MIN.

invernali [een-vair-**nah**-lee] winter dishes.

involtini [een-vol-**tee**-neeh] thin slices of meat or fish spread with a filling and then rolled up.

iota [**yoh**-tah] a stew of beans, bacon and sauerkraut, from Friuli-Venezia Giulia.

ircano [ear-**kah**-noh] Sardinian goat's milk cheese.

issopo [**ee**-soh-poh] hyssop, a strong-tasting herb used in cordials and confectionery.

italico [ee-**tah**-lee-koh] a type of soft cow's milk cheese. Any cheese made in the same way as BEL PAESE is a *tipo italico*.

IVA *Imposta sul Valore Aggiunto*, the Italian equivalent of VAT (UK); consumption tax.

Jambon de Bosses [**zom**-bon duh **boss**] PROSCIUTTO CRUDO flavoured with juniper berries and herbs, from Valle d'Aosta.

jota see iota.

kaiserschmarrn [keye-zair-shmarn] a Trentino-Alto Adige dessert of Austrian origin consisting of fried shredded pancake sprinkled with powdered sugar and served with stewed fruit.

kaminwurzen [kam-een-**voorts**-en] smoked pork sausages from Trentino-Alto Adige.

kasher [**kash**-er] kosher.

knödel [**nuh**-del] see CANEDERLI.

krafi [**krah**-fee] pasta stuffed with cheese, eggs and sugar, from Friuli and Istria.

lacetti see ANIMELLE.

lagane [lah-**gah**-nay] broad pasta noodles with an ancient heritage. APICIUS mentions them; so does the 1st-century Latin poet Horace, who speaks of sitting down to a bowl of *lagane*, chickpeas and leeks. The recipe has not much changed. *Lagane e ciceri* (with chickpeas) and *lagane e porri* (with leeks) can still be found on menus in the south. In Puglia they eat CICERI *e tria*.

Lagrein [lah-**grine**] red-wine grape from the Alto Adige region producing some attractive rosé wines.

laianelle [lay-a-**nell**-ay] RICOTTA-filled RAVIOLI from Molise served with a meat

RAGÙ, traditionally goat, but nowadays other meats are often substituted.

Lambrusco [lam-**broos**-koh] a fizzy red wine mainly made in Emilia-Romagna, from a grape of the same name.

Lamon [la-**mon**] town in the Belluno province of the Veneto, famous for its beans, FAGIOLI *di Lamon*.

lampascione see CIPOLLACCIO.

lampone [lam-**poh**-nay] raspberry.

lampuga [lam-**poo**-gah] dolphin-fish.

lampreda [lam-**pray**-dah] lamprey, either *lampreda di mare* (sea lamprey) or *di fiume* (river lamprey). In ancient times they were drowned in Malmsey wine (MALVASIA)— incidentally the fate that befalls the Duke of Clarence in Shakespeare's *Richard III*. The custom was widespread throughout Europe and it is reasonable to suppose that the lampreys which caused the English king Henry I's 'fatal surfeit' may also have been prepared in this way. Today they are stewed *alla Bordolese*: in the best Bordeaux vintage you can afford.

lampredotto [lam-pray-**doh**-to] in Tuscany, tripe.

lapistra [lah-**pee**-strah] in Calabria, a wild radish.

lardo [**lar**-doh] cured pork fat. *Lardo di Colonnata* is a particularly prized type, from a small town near Carrara (Tuscany). It narrowly escaped extinction under EU hygiene regulations, a near miss with martyrdom that beatified the product and made it a symbol of heroic Italian resistance to bureaucratic tyranny. *Lardo di Arnad*, from Valle d'Aosta, is similarly praised. It too, fell victim to EU legislation when the chestnut-wood barrels in which it was cured were banned. Other regional *lardi* of note include a *lardo al rosmarino* from Piedmont, cured with rosemary and other herbs.

lasagna, lasagne [laz-**ann**-yah, laz-**ann**-yeh] internationally famous pasta dish in which a meat RAGÙ is layered between thin rectangular sheets of pasta prior to being baked in the oven. See also VINCISGRASSI.

lasagnette [laz-ann-**yet**-ay] narrow strips of LASAGNA pasta.

lasca [**lah**-ska] roach (fish).

lattaiolo [lah-**tie**-oh-loh] cinnamon custard.

latte [**lat**-ay] milk.

latte scremato [**lat**-ay skray-**mah**-to] skimmed milk.

latte fritto [**lat**-ay **free**-toh] milk and sugar thickened with corn starch, left to solidify, then cut in rectangular pieces, breaded and fried; a speciality of Liguria.

latterino [lat-ay-**reen**-oh] the sand smelt, a small fish suitable for frying (pl. *latterini*).

lattonzolo [lah-**tonts**-oh-low] a suckling pig, no more than six or seven weeks old.

lattuga [lah-**too**-gah] lettuce.

lauro [la-**oo**-roh] bay. See ALLORO.

lavanda, lavandula [lah-van-da, lah-**van**-doo-lah] lavender, widely used in baking and confectionery.

lavarello [lah-vah-**rell**-oh] whitefish (a freshwater species).

Lazio [**lats**-ee-oh] central region of Italy, site of ancient Etruscan settlements and eventually of the rise, decline and fall of Imperial Rome followed by the steady growth of Christian Rome. Despite all this world-shaping history, the cuisine is simple and local. Bread, cheese, lamb, artichokes and offal are the staples of Lazio cooking. Even the wines are humble, with FRASCATI probably the best known.

leccalecca [lecka-**leck**-ah] an ice lolly, popsicle.

leccia [**letch**-yah] amberjack, an Atlantic fish.

leggero/a [ledge-**ay**-roh] mild, light.

legna [**lane**-yah] wood.

lenticchie [layn-**tee**-kee-ay] lentils. *Lenticchie di Castelluccio*, from the village of the same name in Umbria, are the most famous of all Italian lentils.

lepre [**lay**-pray] hare.

lepudrida [lay-poo-**dree**-da] Sardinian meat and vegetable soup of Spanish origin, similar to *olla podrida* ('rotten pot').

lesso [**less**-oh] simmered; by association boiled meat. *Lesso e pearà*, in the Veneto, is a dish of mixed boiled meats with a purée of vegetables and stale bread.

levistico [lay-**vee**-stee-koh] lovage.

Liber de Coquina the *Book of the Cook*, a 14th-century Latin codex thought to have been written by a Neapolitan. It contains recipes for fish, poultry and desserts, and is full of examples of contemporary gastronomic lore.

licurdia [lee-**koor**-dee-ah] onion soup (Calabria).

Liguria [lee-**goo**-ree-ah] northwestern coastal region of Italy (the port of Genoa is its principal city) known for its fish dishes and for the many varieties of fresh and dried pasta on offer. There is much debate as to what constitutes the perfect Genoese PESTO and many types are on the market. FOCACCIA is typical of the region, as is the chickpea bread known as *farinata*. Ligurian olive oil is much more delicate in flavour than Tuscan—it goes better with fish.

lime [**lee**-may] lime.

limonata [lee-moan-**ah**-tah] lemonade, lemon soda.

limoncello [lee-moan-**chay**-loh] a lemon-based DIGESTIVO made from fragrant southern Italian lemons from around the Gulf of Naples, those from Sorrento being held to be the best. The Amalfi Coast tradition is to serve it in a small, chilled beaker or glass, and this has spread throughout Italy and beyond.

limone [lee-**moan**-ay] lemon.

linguattola [lean-**gwat**-oh-lah] the spotted flounder.

lingue di gatto [lean-gway

dee **gah**-toh] cat's tongues, *langues de chat* biscuits.

lingue di suocera [lean-gway dee **swoh**-chay-rah] 'mother-in-law's tongues', crispy flat GRISSINI, often flavoured with salt and rosemary.

linguine [lean-**gwee**-nay] 'little tongues', pasta strands resembling flattened spaghetti.

Liptauer [le**a**p-tah-wah] a spicy, spreadable sheep's cheese, popular in Trieste but originating in the part of old Austria-Hungary that is now Slovakia.

liquirizia [lee-kwee-**reet**-see-ah] liquorice.

liquori [lee-**kwor**-ee] liqueurs.

liquoroso [lee-kwor-**oh**-zoh] of a wine, fortified.

liscio/a [**leesh**-oh] straight. Of pasta, unridged; of spirits, neat; of water, still.

locanda [loh-**kan**-dah] in theory a simple restaurant, though the term has been taken up by high-end restaurateurs. A *locanda* may be anything from a spit-and-sawdust rural set-up to a sophisticated cosmopolitan venue.

Lombardy northern Italian region well known for its glamorous capital city Milan (home to some of the most famous restaurants in Italy) and for the beauties of its lakes, Como and Maggiore (Lake Garda is split between Lombardy and Veneto). Local produce includes plenty of protein-rich produce, for example GORGONZOLA and TALEGGIO cheese, BRESAOLA (cured beef) and a variety of sausages. The FRANCIACORTA DOCG produces the best wine.

lombata, lombo [lom-**bah**-tah, **lom**-boh] loin (e.g. of beef, veal, pork).

lombatina [lom-bah-**tee**-nah] loin (usually of veal).

lombrichelli [lom-breek-**ell**-ee] 'little earthworms', thick spaghetti-like pasta from Lazio.

lonza [**lont**-sah] pork loin.

lorighittas [lorry-**gee**-tas] braided pasta from Morgongiori in Sardinia.

luccio [**loo**-choh] pike (fish).

luganega [loo-gan-**ay**-gah] (pl. *luganeghe*) a slender pork sausage, sold by length. Its origins are very old: it is recorded in the writings of Latin authors, who call it *lucanica*, after the ancient region of southern Italy corresponding to modern Basilicata.

lumache [loo-**mack**-ay] snails, either the live variety or pasta shapes, also known as *lumachine, lumachelle, luma-chette* and *lumaconi. Lumache di vigna* [dee **vee**-nya] or *lumache di San Giovanni* [dee san-joe-**van**-ee] are said to ward off evil spirits and are eaten in Rome and Lazio on 24th June, the feast of St John the Baptist. The snails are served in a sauce of garlic and tomatoes, to which anchovies and chilli may also be added.

lunette [loo-**net**-ay] half-moon-shaped RAVIOLI.

lunghetti [loon-**gay**-tee] semi-long slender pasta from Emilia-Romagna, known in dialect as *lunghètt*, but more commonly referred to as STROZZAPRETI. A tradi-tional recipe serves them with breadcrumbs and cinnamon.

lupo di mare [**loop**-oh dee **mah**-ray] sea bass.

luppoli [loo-poh-lee] hops.

lusso [**loose**-oh] luxury; *ristorante di lusso*: a five-star restaurant.

maccarello [mack-a-**rell**-oh] mackerel.

maccheroni [mack-ay-**roe**-nee] a pasta of varying shapes and sizes, mainly but not exclusively tubular in shape, native to Sicily and Calabria but widespread throughout southern Italy.

maccù [mack-**oo**] see INC-APRIATA.

macedonia di frutta [mah-chay-**doe**-nee-ah dee **froo**-tah] fruit salad.

macinato/a [mah-chee-**nah**-toh] minced or ground.

mafalde, mafaldine [ma-**fal**-day, ma-fal-**dee**-nay] ribbon-shaped pasta, a kind of LASAGNETTE, widespread in Italy and named after Princess Mafalda, daughter of King Vittorio Emanuele III. Mafalda died in Buchenwald in 1944.

maggiorana [madge-oh-**rahn**-ah] marjoram.

magro [**mah**-groh] lean, not fatty, thin.

maiale [my-**ah**-lay, my-ah-**leen**-oh] pig, pork.

maialino [my-ah-lee-noh] piglet, either a suckling pig (*lattonzolo*), or an animal around a year old, suitable for making PORCHETTA.

maionese [my-oh-**nay**-zay] mayonnaise, in Italy made with eggs and olive oil, sometimes with a squeeze of lemon juice.

mais [may **is**] maize, sweet-corn.

malfatti, malfattini [mal-fat-ee, mal-fat-**ee**-nee] 'badly made' little scraps of pasta, resembling medium to small *gnocchetti*, traditionally served in soups.

malga [**mahl**-ga] mild, creamy summer cheese from the al-

pine regions of Friuli-Venezia Giulia; the *malga* is a wooden hut used by cowherds for shelter, storing equipment and for making cheese.

malloreddus [mall-oh-**redh**-oos] sturdy southern Italian GNOCCHI, curled over on one side and ridged on the other, the better to trap the sauce. Sardinian *malloreddus* are sometimes coloured and flavoured with saffron.

maltagliati [mal-tall-**yah**-tee] 'the badly cut ones', coarsely cut pasta shapes found extensively in Italy, served with a variety of sauces. They are given different names in different regions (see BLECS). In the province of Ferrara they are known as *sguazzabarbuz* ('beard-splatterers') because it is impossible not to eat them messily.

Malvasia [mal-**vah**-zee-ah] dry white wine made from an ancient grape variety of the same name, prevalent in northeast Italy (and in Dalmatia), perhaps an ancient

Greek variety. The old English name is Malmsey.

manate [mah-**nah**-tay] pasta from Vaglio di Basilicata. The paste is kneaded into a ball with egg, then flattened and cut into thin strips.

mandarino [man-dah-**ree**-noh] mandarin orange.

mandili 'nversoi [man-dee-leen-vair-**soy**] 'reversed handkerchiefs', Piedmontese pasta similar to TORTELLINI but made without egg. They are filled with sausage and sweetbreads.

mandili di sea [man-**dee**-lee dee **say**-ah] 'silk handker-chiefs', thin squares of pasta typical of Liguria.

mandorla [**man**-dor-lah] almond (pl. *mandorle*). Two varieties are grown: *dolci*, the sweet almonds used in confectionery, and *mandorle amare*, the bitter almonds used in liqueurs.

maneghi [man-**ay**-gee] sweet potato GNOCCHI from the Veneto, elongated rather than round.

manfricoli [man-**free**-koh-lee] a kind of spaghetti made with FARRO flour.

manicotti [man-ee-**kot**-ee] 'muffs', pasta in the form of sections of tube.

mantecato/a [man-tay-**kat**-oh] creamed, as in the BAC-CALÀ *mantecato* of Venice.

manto [**man**-toh] a coating or crust.

manzo [**mant**-soh] beef.

maraconda see MARICONDA.

maracuja [mah-rah-**koo**-yah] passion fruit.

marasche [mah-**rass**-kay] Morello cherries.

Marche [**mar**-kay] central Italian region with an Adriatic coastline, known for its picturesque towns and cities such as Urbino and Ancona. The coastal cuisine of the Marche centres on *brodetti*, soups that exploit the seasonal variety of fish. Inland, the *Marchigiani* are keen carnivores, and keen contenders in Italy's widespread manufacture of SALUMI. The cured sausages of the region are excellent, and chunks of sausage and lard, as well as cheese, are typically stuck into the soft bread called *crescia*. VERDICCHIO is the region's dry white wine.

Margherita [mar-gay-**ree**-ta] Queen of Italy (1851–1926) consort of Umberto I. The Pizza Margherita is said to have been named after her by its creator, a Neapolitan pizza chef called Raffaele Esposito. The ingredients, herbs, MOZZARELLA and tomatoes, echo the Italian national colours, green, white and red.

margherite [mar-gay-**ree**-tay] 'daisies', a pasta shape.

mariconda [mah-ree-**kon**-dah] a bread dumpling, typical of Mantua, often served in broth (pl. *mariconde*).

marinaia, marinara, alla [mah-ree-**neye**-ah, mah-ree-**nah**-rah] 'sailor style'. Most such dishes would originally have been made by fishermen, and thus use ingredients which they could have taken with them on voyages. Anchovies, capers, olives and other salted items predominate.

marinato/a [mah-ree-**nah**-toh] marinaded.

Marinetti *see box overleaf.*

maritozzi [mah-ree-**tots**-ee] sweet buns (Rome).

marmellata [mar-may-**lah**-ta] jam.

marmitta [mar-**mee**-tah] a pot or stockpot.

marrone [mah-**roe**-nay] chestnut (pl. *marroni*).

Marsala [mar-**sah**-lah] a fortified wine from western Sicily, made either with red-skinned grapes (dark Marsala) or white-skinned grapes (the amber-coloured Marsala). It is often drunk with cheese, and is frequently used in cooking.

Martini a vermouth first produced by the Martini & Rossi distillery in Turin. The dry Martini (vermouth and gin) was invented in New York in the early 20th century.

marubini [mah-roo-**bee**-nee] PASTA RIPIENA typical of Cremona, Lombardy.

Marinetti, Filippo (1876–1944)

Italian artist, progenitor of the Futurist movement in Italy, a vigorous debunker of the bourgeois values and habits he thought had infected Italian life over the centuries as a result of foreign, chiefly French, Austrian and British, influence, Marinetti advocated a series of sweeping reforms, not only in art and politics but also in gastronomy. His uncompromising nationalism found favour with Mussolini and for a while his ideas were influential. Though the Futurist recipes devised by Marinetti and his fellow artists were frequently bizarre (e.g. SALAME cooked in black coffee with *eau de cologne*), he gained recognition as one of the first public figures to challenge the time-honoured Italian reverence for pasta. It was 'no food for fighters' he maintained. Furthermore, it was 'anti-virile' and no man with a stomach 'weighty and encumbered' with spaghetti could hope to make love to a woman as a true Italian should. Whatever nutritional merit these proscriptions may have had, they never caught on, though his attempts to revise the language and rid it of foreign contaminants such as 'cocktail' are interesting. Marinetti came up with the neologism *polibibita* ('multi-drink', Italian-sounding enough, although the first part in fact derives from the Greek *poly*). Other Marinettisms include *guidopalato* ('palate-guide', i.e. head waiter) and *guerra in letto* ('war-in-the-bed', i.e. an aphrodisiac).

maruzze [mah-**roo**-tsay] small snails.

marzapane [marts-ah-**pan**-ay] 1. marzipan; 2. in Piedmont, a type of pork SALAME.

marzolino [marts-oh-**lee**-noh] soft sheep's cheese traditionally made in the month of March (*marzo*) in the Chianti region in Tuscany.

marzotica [mar-**tsoh**-tee-ka] a Puglian RICOTTA made of a mixture of cow's, sheep's and goat's milk. Used either as a table cheese or for grating.

masaro SEE MAZORO.

mascarpone [mas-kar-**poh**-nay] creamy-textured fresh cow's milk cheese used for preparing creams and cakes.

masseria [mass-ay-**ree**-ah] a wine or oil producing farm.

matasse [ma-**tass**-ay] 'skeins', long pasta noodles manufactured and packaged in bundles. Also known as *nidi*, 'nests'.

matota [ma-**tote**-ah] Piedmontese word for bacon; a kind of SALAME.

matriciana, alla SEE AMATRICIANA.

maturazione [mat-oo-rats-ee-**own**-ay] the maturing process.

mazoro [mats-**or**-oh] wild duck.

mazzafegati [matz-ah-**fay**-gat-ee] Umbrian pork liver sausages, sometimes sweetened with raisins.

mazzancolla [mats-ahn-**kol**-ah] the giant Mediterranean shrimp (*Penaeus kerathurus*).

mazzarelle [mats-ah-**rell**-ay] lamb's offal wrapped in lettuce leaves, a speciality of the Abruzzo.

medaglione [med-al-**yohn**-ay] a medallion or circular fillet.

mela [**may**-lah] apple (pl. *mele*).

melagrana [may-lah-**grah**-na] pomegranate.

melanzana [may-lant-**sah**-nah] (pl. *melanzane*), aubergine, eggplant.

melassa [may-**lass**-ah] molasses.

melegueta [may-lay-**gway**-tah] SEE AFRAMOMO.

melone [may-**loan**-ay] melon.

menietti [main-ee-**ett**-ee] a PASTINA native to Liguria.

mennuli [men-oo-lee] almonds (Sicily).

menta [**main**-tah] mint.

menuzze [may-**noot**-say] a type of PASTINA typically used in fish broth. Also known as *tretarielle*.

Meraner Leiten [meh-**rahn**-

er **lie**-ten] a light red wine from Merano in Alto Adige.

merca see ZIBBA.

mercato [mair-**kah**-to] market.

meringa [may-**ring**-ah] meringue. *Meringata* is meringue pie.

merlano [mair-**lan**-oh] whiting (fish).

merletti [mair-**let**-ee] pasta pieces shaped like lace, used in soups or salads.

merli [**mair**-lee] blackbirds.

merluzzo [mayor-**loots**-oh] fresh cod. Also the name for hake.

mescciüa [mes-**chü**-ah] Ligurian soup of chickpeas, beans and wheat grains.

mescuetille [mess-kwet-**eel**-ay] square, thickish lumps of pasta from Puglia.

mescuotte [mess-**kwot**-ay] sweet, aniseed-flavoured loaves from Basilicata.

mesi [**may**-zee] months.

messicani [messy-**kan**-ee] a pasta shape: 'Mexican hats', resembling sombreros.

mestolone [mess-toh-**loan**-ee] shoveler (duck).

metodo Charmat [**may**-toad-oh shar-**mah**] method of producing sparkling wine wherein the secondary fermentation takes place in a steel tank rather than in individual bottles, as in *méthode champenoise*. Also known as *metodo italiano*, the Charmat technique is usually used for ASTI SPUMANTE and PROSECCO.

mezzalune [medz-ah-**loon**-ay] half-moon pasta shapes.

mezzano [med-**zah**-noh] moderately aged (cheese).

mezze maniche [**med**-zay-**mahn**-ee-kay] 'half sleeves', a short tubular pasta shape.

mezzo/a [**med**-zoh] half.

michetta [mee-**ket**-ah] type of bread shaped like a rosette, with 'petals' surrounding a round centre. Also known as *rosetta*.

microonde [mee-kroh-**on**-day] microwave oven.

midolline [me-doll-**ee**-nee] fragments of pasta resembling melon seeds.

midollo [me-**doll**-oh] bone-marrow.

miele [me-**ail**-ay] honey.

mignaculis [mean-**yah**-koo-lees] pasta used in soup (Friuli).

miglio [mee-**lee**-oh] millet.

milanese, alla [mee-lah-**nay**-zay] 1. cooked with beef marrow, white wine, saffron and PARMESAN (RISOTTO); 2. breaded veal schnitzel, see COSTOLETTA.

millefanti [mee-lay-**fan**-tee] tiny strands of pasta served in broth.

millefoglie [mee-lay-**foh**-lee-ay] puff pastry, millefeuille.

milza [meel-tsah] spleen.

minestra, minestrone [mee-**nay**-strah, mee-nay-**stroh**-nay] a thick soup, usually made with vegetables though it may contain meat or poultry and be based on either a vegetable or meat stock. Rice, pasta or another staple is often used to augment it. The word is derived from the Latin *ministrare*, to serve, and therefore means simply 'that which is served', appropriate

given its variety of incarnations, the recipe being usually based on what is in the larder.

minne di vergine [**minn**-ay dee **vair**-jee-nay] 'virgin's breasts', Sicilian iced cream-filled buns.

minuich [mean-oo-**eek**] tubular pasta from Puglia and Basilicata, similar to MACCHERONI. Also known as *minnicchi*.

mirtilli [meer-**till**-ee] bilberries, blueberries.

mirto [**meer**-toh] myrtle.

mirtù [mere-**too**] a Sardinian myrtleberry DIGESTIVO.

mischiglio [miss-**kee**-lee-oh] pasta from Basilicata, traditionally made from barley, chickpea, broad bean and oat flours mixed with wheat.

missultini, missultit [miss-ool-**teen**-ee, miss-ool-**teet**] sun- or wind-dried AGONI from the Lake Como area.

misticanza [mees-tee-**kahn**-tsa] mixed leaf salad.

misto/a [**mees**-toh] mixed.

Mistrà [mees-**trah**] an anise-flavoured liqueur, a good AM-

MAZZACAFFÈ. A reliable Mistrà is made by Varnelli, from the Marche.

mocetta [moh-**chet**-ah] cured goat's meat (traditionally chamois), made in the Valle d'Aosta.

moddizzosu [mod-its-oh-**su**]a soft FOCACCIA-type bread from Sardinia.

moeche [**mweck**-ay] see MOLECA.

moleca [mole-**ay**-kah] (pl. *moleche*, also *moeche*). Crabs caught in the Venetian lagoon towards the end of April when they are changing their shells, which are therefore soft and succulent. The crabs are deep-fried whole in olive oil.

moleche see MOLECA.

Molinara [moll-ee-**nah**-rah] red grape used as part of the VALPOLICELLA and BARDOLINO blends of Northern Italy.

Molise [moll-**ee**-zay] the second-smallest Italian region (after Valle d'Aosta), mainly mountainous with a short coastline (40km) on the Adriatic. Its gastronomic heritage is firmly rooted in its pastoral history, and has much in common with that of Abruzzo (the two were a single region until the mid-1960s). There is a wide variety of sheep's milk cheese and an abundant use of chilli in the preservation and cooking of meat.

molle [**moll**-ay] soft.

mollica di pane [**moll**-ee-kah dee **pah**-nay] breadcrumbs.

molluschi [moh-**loos**-key] shellfish.

monarda [mon-**ard**-ah] bergamot.

Monica [**moan**-ee-kah] Sardinian red grape producing light-coloured medium-flavoured reds.

Montalcino [mont-al-**chee**-noh] town in Tuscany famed for its wine. See BRUNELLO.

Montasio [moan-**tah**-zee-oh] an alpine cow's milk cheese made in the Friuli region.

montasù [mon-tah-**soo**] a soft, mild-tasting bread roll with an almost creamy-textured crust and scroll-like ends, typical of Venice.

Montepulciano [mon-tay-pull-**chah**-noh] red-wine grape used to produce the fruity, intense Montepulciano d'Abruzzo. It is a grape variety and not to be confused with the Tuscan town of Montepulciano, known for its Vino Nobile.

montone [mon-**tone**-ay] mutton.

mora [**more**-ah] blackberry (pl. *more*).

morchella [more-**keh**-lah] morel mushroom (pl. *morchelle*).

morena [more-**ay**-nah] see MURENA.

Morlacco [more-**lack**-oh] also known as *morlac*, a creamy cow's milk cheese from the northern Veneto.

moro [**more**-oh] blood orange.

mortadella [more-tah-**dell**-ah] a smoked, sweetish, aromatic pork sausage from Bologna and Emilia-Romagna, flavoured with black pepper, myrtle berries, nutmeg, coriander, pistachio nuts and olives. *Mortadella di Campotosto* is a hard pork SALUME from the Abruzzo, popularly known as *coglioni di mulo* ('mule's testicles').

morzeddhu see MURSEDDU.

moscardino [moss-kar-**deen**-oh] 1. the musky octopus; 2. a dormouse, eaten with relish in the time of APICIUS (roasted with honey and spices).

Moscato [moss-**kah**-toh] the Muscat grape, used mainly to make sparkling or sweet wines. There are many varieties, and man has been vinifying them for a long time. The legendary King Midas of Phrygia (in modern Turkey), who was said to be able to turn everything to gold, apparently drank Muscat. The main varieties grown in Italy are *Moscato bianco* and *Moscato giallo*. The first is grown in Piedmont (where it is used in ASTI SPUMANTE) and the second in Trentino-Alto Adige, where it is used to produce dessert wines. Moscato wines are also produced in Sicily.

mosciame [mosh-**ah**-meh] also spelled *mosciamme* and *musciamme*. Originally a cut of dried dolphin meat; today tuna has replaced dolphin.

mostaccioli [moss-**tatch**-oh-lee] diamond-shaped biscuits, originally cooked with grape must. Today they are often coated in chocolate.

mostarda [moss-**tar**-dah] a chutney, made with fruit and mustard-flavoured syrup. A famous example is *Mostarda di Cremona*, from the city of that name in Lombardy. *Mostarda* is typically served with cold boiled meats. NB: *mostarda* is not the Italian for mustard. That is *senape*.

mostardella [moss-tar-**deh**-lah] a Ligurian beef and pork SALUME.

mosto [**moss**-toh] grape must. *Mosto cotto*, lit. 'cooked must', is must that has been heat-reduced to a thick syrup.

motzetta [mot-**zett**-ah] cured meat, originally mountain

goat (see MOCETTA). Nowadays other meats are used. *Motzetta bovina* is cured beef.

mozzarella [mots-ah-**rell**-ah] a soft, white cheese made from the milk of water buffaloes and preserved in brine. When fresh, the centre is a delectable mix of crumbly and runny textures. It is never rubbery.

'mpanatigghi [oom-pah-nah-**tee**-gee] *dolci di carne*, literally 'sweet meats': Sicilian pastries filled with nuts, chocolate, sugar, spices and beef.

'mparrettati [oom-par-ett-**ah**-tee] long pasta straws.

muggine [moo-**jeen**-ay] grey mullet.

mula [**moo**-lah] pork SALUME from Piedmont.

murena [moo-**ray**-nah] the moray eel.

murice [moo-**ree**-chay] the murex, a shellfish prized in antiquity as the source of purple dye for imperial robes. *Murici* are eaten today as an ANTIPASTO or with pasta.

murseddu [moor-**sedh**-oo]

also *mursiello, morzeddhu*, Calabrian stewed tripe.

mustica [moo-stee-kah] a Calabrian pâté of salted baby sardines and chilli. Served on bread as an ANTIPASTO.

muschiata [moos-key-**ah**-tah] the muscovy duck.

muscisca [moo-**shees**-kah] a Puglian speciality consisting of air-dried strips of pork, mutton or beef (formerly goat), well seasoned.

muscolo [moose-**koh**-loh] stewing meat from the hind leg.

musèt, musetto [moo-**zet**, moo-**zet**-oh] a sausage made of meat from the pig's head (Friuli-Venezia Giulia).

nasello [nah-**zell**-oh] hake.

nastrini [nas-**tree**-nee] 'ribbons', a pasta shape.

natalin, natalini [nah-tah-**leen**, nah-tah-**lee**-nee] the 'Christmas *maccheroni*' of Genoa, long, smooth PENNE served in broth.

navoni [nah-**voh**-nee] turnips.

'ncapriata see INCAPRIATA.

'ndocca 'ndocca [oon-**dock**-ah oon-**dock**-ah] in Abruzzo, a stew of cheap cuts of pig, including the blood.

'ndugghia see INDUGGHIA.

'nduja [oon-**doo**-yah] Calabrian spreadable sausage made of pork offal and chilli.

Nebbiola [nay-bee-**oh**-lah] Piedmontese grape, one of the most venerated Italian varieties, used in BAROLO and BARBARESCO. The name Nebbiolo means 'little fog' and refers to the autumn mists characteristic of the area.

Negroamaro [nay-grow-ah-**mahr**-oh] red-wine grape from Puglia used to produce dark, rustic wines such as Salice Salentino.

Negroni [nay-**grow**-nee] a cocktail of gin, vermouth and bitters, typically CAMPARI.

nepitella [nay-pee-**tell**-ah] calamint.

nepitelle [nay-pee-**tell**-ay] little pastry pies filled with nuts and figs (Calabria)

nero/a [**nay**-roh] black.

Nero d'Avola [**nay**-roh dah-**voh**-lah] a red-wine grape native to Sicily, used to make rich, plummy wines.

nero di seppia [**nay**-roh dee **sep**-ee-ah] cuttlefish ink.

nervetti [nair-**vet**-ee] calf sinews and ligaments, served as a snack or ANTIPASTO.

nespola [**nay**-spoh-lah] medlar. *Nespola giapponese* is a loquat.

nettarina [nay-tah-ree-nah] nectarine.

'nfigghiulata [oon-feeg-you-**lah**-tah] a kind of Sicilian pasty, filled either with sweetened RICOTTA, or, in the savoury version, with cheese, sausage and PANCETTA.

'ngritoli [oon-greet-ee-**oh**-lee] a PASTINA from Lazio.

nidi [**nee**-dee] 'nests'.

nocchette [nock-**ett**-ay] 1. baked dried figs stuffed with walnuts or almonds (Calabria); 2. a kind of FARFALLE.

nocciola [**notch**-oh-lah] a hazelnut (pl. *nocciole*).

noce [**notch**-ay] 1. walnut (pl. *noci*); 2: a cut of meat from the top of the leg.

noce di cocco [**notch**-ay dee cock-oh] coconut.

noce moscata [**notch**-ay moss-**kaht**-ah] nutmeg.

Nocino [notch-**ee**-noh] bittersweet liqueur that purists insist should be made from green walnuts picked by barefooted, bareheaded virgins from Emilia-Romagna on the night of 23rd June, the eve of the feast of St John the Baptist. In the real world Nocino is produced as far afield as New Zealand and the Napa Valley with minimal emphasis placed on either chastity or the cult of St John.

nodini di vitello [noh-**dee**-nee dee vee-**teh**-lo] veal rib chops.

Norcia [**nor**-cha] town in Umbria known for its pork products and its truffles. A butcher's shop is often still called a *norcineria*.

Norma, alla [**nor**-ma] *pasta alla Norma* is a Sicilian dish featuring a rich sauce of aubergine, tomato, basil and cheese. It was named in honour of the opera *Norma*

(1831) by the Catanian composer Vincenzo Bellini. Though he had in mind the appropriately named soprano Giuditta Pasta when he created the title role, Bellini's opera is about love, betrayal and filial loyalty rather than gastronomic ecstasy.

nostrano, nostrale [nos-**trah**-noh, nos-**trah**-lay] local, e.g. *vino nostrano*: local wine.

novello [no-**vel**-oh] of wine, young, of the new vintage, comparable to the French Beaujolais Nouveau.

'nsacaragatti see FRASCARELLI.

'ntruppicc [oon-**troo**-peek] (Sicily) a RAGÙ of finely diced pork and lamb.

nuglia see INDUGGHIA.

nunnatu [noo-**nah**-too] in Sicily and Calabria, tiny fish that have only just reached maturity (the word means 'new-born'; *neonato*). They are usually served deep-fried.

nuraghe [noo-**rah**-gay] a conical megalithic tower house constructed by the prehistoric Nuragic tribes of Sardinia.

The name *nuraghe*, *nuraghi*, or *nuraghes* is commonly found in Sicilian dishes, e.g. *zuppa dei Nuraghi*.

Nuragus [noo-**rah**-goose] white-wine grape from southern Sardinia, used to make light, dry wines.

'nzuddi [oon-**zoo**-dhee] in the south of Italy, little biscuits similar to MOSTACCIOLI.

oca [**ock**-ah] goose.

occhio di bue [**ock**-ee-oh dee **boo**-ay] 1. a fried egg (lit. 'bull's eye'); 2. a shortcake biscuit with a jam centre.

occhi di lupo [**ock**-ee dee **loo**-poh] 'wolf's eyes', a smooth, tubular pasta. The size of the cut can vary, and so can the name: *occhi di elefante* '(elephant's eyes') are large tubes; *occhi di passero* ('sparrow's eyes') are tiny ones.

occhiata [ocky-**ah**-tah] a species of sea bream.

odori [oh-**dore**-ee] lit. 'scents', by association, herbs.

offelle [oh-**fell**-ay] 1. little oval-shaped shortbread biscuits; 2. jam-filled shortbread tarts; 3. in Friuli-Venezia Giulia, RAVIOLI filled with meat, sausage and spinach.

olio [oh-lee-oh] oil; *olio di oliva* = olive oil (*see box below*).

olio santo [oh-lee-oh **san**-toh] literally 'holy oil': olive oil flavoured with chilli.

olive [oh-**lee**-vay] olives, the fruits of the olive tree, pickled in brine to make them edible. *Olive ascolane* (or *all'ascolana*), with a meat stuffing, dipped in egg and breadcrumbs and deep fried, are a speciality of the Marche.

Olive oil

Olive groves have been planted throughout the Mediterranean since ancient times, though planting and production in Italy became increasingly intensive and systematic under Roman domination. This partly explains why the Sabine hills in Lazio outside Rome remain Italy's most revered and widely publicised source of fine oils, though it would be a mistake to ignore the many regional oil varieties throughout Italy. Oil is like wine, varying enormously in taste from area to area. Olives, like grapes, are fruit, and as such they take on characteristics determined by soil, climate and the manner in which they are cared for: Ligurian oils are delicate, Calabrian pungent, Tuscan robust and so on. The publisher Slow Food Editore releases an annual guide, *La Guida agli Extravergini*, in which hundreds of Italian oils are reviewed having been tasted by a panel of experts. The terms 'extra virgin' and 'virgin' refer to the acidity of an oil, extra virgin having no more than 0.8 percent acidity and virgin oil no more than 2 percent. These oils are known as cold-pressed oils, 'cold' because they have not been subjected to the various refining processes essential in mass production, all of which require heat. Heat destroys flavour,

which is why a cold pressed extra-virgin or virgin oil from a respected FRANTOIO, replete with a unique regional flavour, is so highly prized.

olivette [oh-lee-**vet**-ay] little olives.

omaso [oh-**mah**-zoh] tripe.

ombelichi di venere [om-**bay**-lick-oh dee **vay**-nay-ray] 'navels of Venus', another name for TORTELLINI.

ombra [**ohm**-brah] literally, a 'shadow', a small glass of wine. The name is said to derive from Venice, where wine sellers set up their stalls in the shadow of the bell-tower of San Marco.

ombrina di scoglio [om-**bree**-nah dee **skoh**-lyoh] see CORVINA.

ombrina leccia [om-**bree**-nah **letch**-ah] leerfish.

omelette [oh-may-**leh**-tay] a French-style omelette, fried and folded over on itself.

omento [oh-**main**-toh] caul, the fatty membrane enclosing the intestines of an animal. Also known as *rete* ('net'), it is used for wrapping FEGATELLI.

onda, all [**on**-dah] of RISOTTO, cooked so that it is neither stiff nor sloppy, and the surface can be made to peak, like a wave ('*onda*').

opa [**oh**-pah] southern name for BOGA.

orata [oh-**rah**-tah] gilt-head bream.

orecchiette [oh-reck-**yet**-ay] little ears', a pasta shape.

origano [oh-ree-**gah**-no] oregano.

Ornellaia [or-nell-**eye**-ah] dry red wine from BOLGHERI, one of the SUPERTUSCANS, made using Bordeaux grape varieties.

orsetti [ore-**set**-ee] 'little bears', a pasta or biscuit shape for children.

Orvieto [or-vee-**ay**-toh] town in Umbria known for its wine. See GRECHETTO.

orzata [ort-**sah**-tah] barley water, almond-milk.

orzo [**ort**-soh] 1. barley; 2. PASTINA shaped like barley grains, used in soups and salads.

osei [oh-**zay**-ee] in northern Italian dialect (Lombardy and the Veneto) songbirds, such as the lark or thrush, traditionally served with POLENTA. Shooting restrictions and a scarcity of birds have meant that nowadays the dish is undergoing a metamorphosis as a dessert. Don't be surprised to see *polenta e osei* served as a mound of sweetened dough topped by chocolate birds. See also UCCELLI SCAPPATI.

Orecchiette, 'little ears' of pasta.

ostia [**os**-tee-ah] a wafer. The term derives from the 'Host', or Communion bread.

ossobuco [oh-so-**boo**-koh] a Milanese speciality, known in dialect as *oss buss*. It consists of sliced veal shank, on the bone with the bone marrow still inside. The name means 'hollow bone' (*osso* = bone, *buco* = hole). True *ossobuco* is cooked *in bianco* (without tomatoes), is braised slowly and flavoured with GREMOLATA towards the end of cooking.

osteria [oss-tay-**ree**-ah] tavern or inn, a simple restaurant.

ostrica [oss-tree-kah] oyster (pl. *ostriche*).

ova chi curcuci [**oh**-vah kee koor-**koo**-chee] eggs and pork rind fried in dripping (Calabria).

ovino [oh-**vee**-noh] sheep.

paccheri [**pack**-air-ee] short, fat pasta tubes from Naples, either stuffed or served with RAGÙ.

paciugo [patch-**oo**-go] *paciugo di gelato* is an ice cream 'mess' from Liguria, a combination of ice creams of various flavours, fresh or dried fruit and Morello cherry syrup.

paccozze [pack-**ot**-say] in Molise, egg-pasta sheets the size of one's palm (*pacca* = slap), cooked in milk and served with a lamb RAGÙ.

padella [pah-**dell**-ah] frying pan.

pagello [pah-**dell**-ah] sea bream.

paglia e fieno [**pal**-ya ay fee-**ay**-noh] literally, 'straw and hay', a combination of white and green, e.g. TAGLIA-TELLE made with and without spinach.

pagnotta [pan-**yot**-ah] a savoury loaf. Also *pagnottina*.

pagro [**pah**-gro] sea bream

pajata [pa-**yah**-tah] a Roman dish featuring the intestines of an unweaned calf. The milk is left inside and cooked with the intestines, which are chopped up and served with RIGATONI and a tomato sauce.

palline [pal-**ee**-nay] small pasta pellets, suitable for long cooking.

palline di riso [pal-**ee**-nay dee **ree**-zoh] rice balls, a variant on ARANCINI

pallott' [pah-**lot**] fried cheese balls (Abruzzo).

palomba, palombaccio [pal-om-bah, pal-om-**batch**-oh] wood pigeon.

palombo [pal-**om**-boh] dogfish.

palumma [pal-**oo**-mah] in Sicily, a pigeon.

pampanella [pam-pan-**ell**-ah] 1. a fresh cheese, traditionally wrapped in vine leaves (Abruzzo); 2. roast pork.

pancetta [pan-**chayt**-ah] salt-cured pork belly.

pancotto [pan-**kot**-oh] 'cooked bread', a soup, with different ingredients according to region, but always thickened with stale bread.

pan di Spagna [**pan** dee **span**-yah] sponge cake.

pandolce [pan-**doll**-chay] a sweet bread made with raisins, pine nuts and candied peel; a fruit loaf.

pandoro, pan d'oro [pan-**doh**-roh] a sweet brioche-style bread shaped like a flat-topped cone, popular around Christmas and New Year. Originally from Verona but widely produced throughout Italy.

pane [**pah**-nay] bread.

pane di Spagna SEE PAN DI SPAGNA.

pane dorato [**pah**-nay doh-**rah**-toh] literally, 'gilded bread': eggy bread (like French toast but not sweet) or fried bread.

pane grattugiatto [**pah**-nay

grah-too-**jah**-toh] 'grated bread'; breadcrumbs.

pane raffermo [**pah**-nay rah-**fair**-mo] stale bread, the basis of many traditional recipes.

panelle [pah-**nell**-ay] Sicilian chickpea fritters.

panera genovese [pah-**nay**-ra je-noh-**vay**-zay] coffee-flavoured cream, served chilled.

panettone [pan-eh-**tone**-ay] the well-known Milanese brioche-style loaf, filled with candied fruit and peel and traditionally eaten at Christmas. The name simply means 'big loaf' but a legend has grown up attributing the name to a certain Toni, a scullion in the household of Duke Lodovico Sforza in the 15th century. During an elaborate banquet the planned dessert was overcooked and spoiled. The resourceful Toni threw together a hotchpotch of bread, butter, candied fruit and raisins. The result, served with some trepidation by the butler, was ecstatically received by Lodovico's guests.

panforte [pan-**fore**-tay] a dense cake filled with dried fruits, nuts and spices, a speciality in Tuscany, particularly Siena.

pangiallo [pan-**jall**-oh] 'yellow' bread, a rich fruitcake from Lazio made with raisins, nuts and spices.

panino [pah-**nee**-noh] a small bread roll; by association, a sandwich (pl. *panini*).

panissa [pah-**niss**-ah] 1. in Liguria a kind of POLENTA made of chickpea flour; 2. in Piedmont a risotto with pork and beans.

pan melato [pan-may-**lah**-toh] spiced honey buns.

panna [**pan**-ah] cream; *panna montata* = whipped cream.

panna cotta [**pan**-ah-**cot**-ah] a popular dessert made by simmering cream, sugar and vanilla, adding gelatin, and pouring into moulds to set.

pannerone [pan-air-**own**-ay] creamy cow's milk cheese with a texture similar to GORGONZOLA.

panpepato [pan-pay-**pah**-toh]

a heavy cake similar to PAN-
FORTE but with the addition of
chocolate and black pepper
(hence *pepato*; 'peppered').
It is traditionally claimed by
Ferrara but is served throughout Italy during Christmas
and Epiphany.

pansotti [pan-**sot**-ee] Ligurian
pasta triangles often stuffed
with chard and served in a
walnut sauce (*salsa di noci*).

panunta [pan-**oon**-tah] stale
or dry bread rubbed with olive oil and garlic. Also known
as FETT'UNTA.

panuria, in [pan-oo-ree-ah]
breaded.

panzanella [pants-ah-**nell**-
ah] a simple Tuscan salad
of bread, onions, basil and
tomatoes dressed with oil and
wine vinegar. The tricolor effect of white bread, red tomatoes and green basil imparts
a patriotic air to the dish.
Count Bettino RICASOLI is said
to have served *panzanella* to
King Vittorio Emanuele II in
1865, during a royal visit to
the Ricasoli estates.

panzerotti [pan-tser-**oh**-tee]
filled, deep-fried pasties.

papalina [pap-ah-**lean**-ah]
sprat (pl. *papaline*).

papero [**pap**-er-oh] duck.

pappa [**pah**-pah] mush,
pottage; in Tuscany, *pappa
al pomodoro* is a version of
PANCOTTO in which tomatoes
predominate.

pappardelle [pah-par-**del**-ay]
strips or ribbons of egg pasta
typically served with a meat
or mushroom sauce. Known
as *paparele* in the Veneto and
paspadelle in the Marche.

pappare [pah-**ar**-ay] to gobble
or 'nosh' in Tuscan dialect.

pappicci [pah-**pee**-chee]
sturdy noodles from the
Abruzzo, typically served in
a simple tomato sauce with
grated cheese.

parago [pah-**rah**-goh] a type
of bream (pl. *paraghi*).

pardulas [par-**doo**-las]
sun-shaped sweet cheese
cakes from Sardinia, served
at Easter and similar to the
Greek *kalitsounia*.

Parma [**Par**-mah] town in

Emilia-Romagna which gives its name to parmesan cheese and Parma ham (see PARMIGIANO and PROSCIUTTO). Acqua di Parma is also a local product, but it is a perfume, not a kind of mineral water.

parmesan see PARMIGIANO.

parmigiana [par-mee-**jan**-ah] *melanzane alla parmigiana* are layers of sliced fried aubergine, tomato sauce and cheese, baked in the oven.

Parmigiano Reggiano [par-mee-**jan**-oh redge-**ah**-noh] Parmesan, the well-known and liberally-used flaky, hard cow's milk cheese, often grated over pasta but also eaten in shavings with PROSCIUTTO, drizzled with oil. Genuine *Parmigiano Reggiano* is produced only from milk obtained within a defined geographical area. The cows eat locally-grown feed and no artificial fermenting agents are used to make the cheese. Certified and attested cheese will have the DOP markings on the rind.

partenopea, alla [par-tayn-oh-**pay**-ah] Neapolitan style, from Parthenope, the ancient Greek colony that preceded Naples.

pasimata [pah-zee-**mah**-tah] a Tuscan Easter cake, filled with raisins, a kind of giant hot cross bun.

passata [pas-**ah**-tah] a purée, e.g. *passata di pomodoro*.

passatelli [pas-ah-**tell**-ee] worm-shaped pasta made of breadcrumbs, egg and cheese, shaped by squeezing the dough through a special crusher like a giant garlic press, then cooked in broth.

passato/a [pah-**sah**-toh] mashed.

passera pianuzza [pah-say-rah pee-ah-**noo**-tsah] flounder.

passito [pah-**see**-toh] a sweet wine made from grapes that are left to dry (traditionally on straw) before being pressed, thus increasing the sugar content of the must.

passoline [pah-soh-**lee**-nay] black Sicilian raisins.

pasta [**pah**-stah]. The quintessential Italian staple: dough made with a variety of flours mixed with water, sometimes also using egg, the basis of an infinite variety of traditional and regional dishes.

Pasta basics

Pasta comes in many variations of the basic forms, which are *pasta lunga* ('long' pastas such as SPAGHETTI and TAGLIATELLE), *pasta corta* ('short', shaped or moulded pastas such as FARFALLE or PENNE) and *pasta ripiena* (filled pastas such as RAVIOLI). Italians call main course pasta dishes *pastasciutta*, 'dry' pasta, to distinguish them from *pasta in brodo*, pasta of a smaller cut and design used in soups: tiny pasta of the kind commonly used in soup is known as *pastina*. *Pasta all'uovo* is made with egg. *Pasta integrale* is wholemeal pasta.

---

pasta corta [**kor**-tah] see *Pasta basics, above.*

pasta e fagioli [**pahs**-tay-**fadge**-oh-lee] a soup of pasta and haricot beans, typical of the Veneto.

pasta filata [fee-**lah**-tah] not pasta, but a cheese-making technique resulting in strings or *file* [**fee**-lay], as in MOZZARELLA.

pasta frolla [**froh**-lah] shortcrust pastry.

pasta grattata, pasta grattugiata [grah-**tah**-tah, grah-too-**jah**-tah] tiny pasta fragments made by forcing dough through a grater and crumbling it into tiny pieces.

pasta lunga [**loon**-gah] see *Pasta basics, above.*

pasta reale [ray-**ah**-lay] literally 'royal' pasta, which can be either 1. marzipan; or 2. dumplings served in broth.

pasta ripiena [ree-pee-**ay**-nah] see *Pasta basics, opposite.*

pasta sfoglia [**sfol**-yah] puff pastry.

pasta strappata [strah-**pah**-

tah] 'torn' pasta, shredded roughly into the cooking pot.

pasta verde [**vair**-day] green pasta, the dough mixed with chopped or puréed spinach.

pastarazzi [pah-stah-**rat**-see] either professionals who take photographs of food for magazines; or amateur bloggers who obsessively photograph their dinners.

pastasciutta [pas-tah-**shoo**-tah] *see Pasta basics, opposite.*

paste di mandorle [**pah**-stay dee **man**-dore-lay] macaroons.

pastella [pah-**stell**-ah] batter.

pasticceria [pah-stee-chay-**ree**-ah] confectioner, confectionery.

pasticcino [pah-stee-**chee**-noh] cake, pastry, tart (pl. *pasticcini*).

pasticcio [pah-**stee**-choh] a pie, in the sense of a shepherd's pie; an oven-baked dish of mixed ingredients, often including pasta.

pastiera [pah-stee-**air**-rah] a RICOTTA pie, often with currants or candied fruit.

pastina [pah-**stee**-nah] *see Pasta basics, opposite.*

pastinaca [pah-stee-**nahk**-ah] parsnip (pl. *pastinache*).

pastine minute [pah-**stee**-nay mee-**noo**-tay] PASTINA.

pastissada [pah-stee-**sah**-dah] a stew of the Veneto region, either of horsemeat (*pastissada de caval*) or beef (*manzo*).

pasto [**pah**-stoh] a meal, c.f. the English 'repast'; hence *antipasto*, 'before the meal', an *hors d'oeuvre*.

pasutice [paz-oo-**tee**-chay] wide noodles.

patacuc [pah-tah-**kook**] also known as CRESC' TAJAT.

patanabò [pah-tah-nah-**boh**] Jerusalem artichoke.

patate [pah-**tah**-tay] potatoes (sing. *patata*). *Patate fritte* are French fries; *patate novelle* are new potatoes.

patatine [pah-tah-**tee**-nay] crisps, potato chips.

patèca [pah-**tay**-kah] watermelon (various dialects).

patellette [pah-tell-**ay**-tay] flat pasta pieces from Abruzzo often served with a sauce

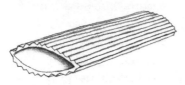

A *penna* (pl. *penne*), a pasta 'quill'.

of onions and PANCETTA.

Paternoster a short prayer, traditionally recited to time the cooking of pasta in the days before people had clocks. By association, the pasta itself, typically a short section of tube.

Pavese, zuppa alla [tsoop-ah alla pah-**vay**-zay] a broth with bread, cheese and an egg in the centre, supposedly served to Francis I of France by a poor peasant woman of Pavia in the 16th century. The king was so impressed that he took the recipe back to France.

pearà [pay-ah-**rah**] see LESSO.

pecora [**pay**-koh-rah] mutton.

pecorino [pay-koh-**ree**-noh] the generic term for hard cheeses made from sheep's milk, of which there are many, varying greatly in fla-vour and texture and subject to rigorous classification. One of the best known is *pecorino romano*, a clean, sharp cheese made in Lazio and parts of Tuscany. *Pecorino sardo* is a pungent Sardinian version.

pecorone [pay-koh-**roh**-nay] 1. a large sheep; 2. a brand of PECORINO from Puglia, market-ed as *il pecorino del ghiottone* ('glutton's *pecorino*').

pelati [pay-**lah**-tee] peeled.

pencarelli [pain-kah-**rell**-ee] long, thick spaghetti-like pas-ta. Also known as *pincarelli*.

penchi [**pain**-key] wide, flat pasta noodles from Umbria.

penne [**pen**-ay] 'quills', famous tubular PASTA CORTA distinctively cut on the bias at both ends. *Penne lisce* [**lee**-shay] are smooth-sided *penne* (not ridged).

pennoni [pen-**noh**-nee] large PENNE, also known as *penne a candela*.

pentola [**pain**-toh-lah] sauce-pan or cooking pot. Dishes are sometimes described as being *alla pentola*, a term suggestive of home cooking.

peoci [pay-**oh**-chee] mussels (Venetian)

pepata di cozze [pay-**pah**-tah dee **cot**-say] poached mussels.

pepato [pay-**pah**-toh] a very sharp Sicilian PECORINO with black peppercorns.

pepe [**pay**-pay] pepper.

pepe verde [**pay**-pay **vair**-day] green pepper.

peperata [pay-pay-**rah**-tah] a sauce made of thickened beef stock, white wine, butter and pepper.

peperonata [pay-pair-oh-**nah**-tah] peppers (often sweet red) braised or sautéed with onion, garlic and tomato.

peperoncino [pay-pair-own-**chee**-noh] the red chilli pepper. Originally introduced to Europe by Columbus, it is a much-loved ingredient in Italian regional cuisine, the best being grown in Calabria and Basilicata. Also known as *diavolillo*, and in Sicily as or *pipi ardenti*.

peperone [pay-pair-**own**-ay] (pl. *peperoni*) red, green or yellow peppers; bell peppers; capsicum.

peposo [pay-**pose**-oh] a Tuscan stew of CHIANINA beef cooked slowly in CHIANTI wine with a large quantity of crushed black peppercorns. Peposo was said to be the favourite food of Brunelleschi. It even has its own website: www.peposo.it.

pera [**pay**-rah] pear (pl. *pere*).

perchia [**pair**-kee-ah] perch.

perciatelli [pair-chah-**tell**-ee] thick strands of spaghetti-like pasta with a hole down the middle.

perlaggio [pair-**ladge**-oh] from the French *perlage*, the size and longevity of bubbles in sparkling wine. A fine wine has plenty of tiny, rapidly-rising streams of bubbles resembling miniature pearl necklaces. A *vino ordinario* has scarce, sparsely-occurring, sluggish bubbles.

pernice [pair-**nee**-cheh] partridge.

persa [**pair**-sah] marjoram.

persico [**pair**-see-koh] fresh-water perch. See also SPIGOLA.

pesca [**pays**-ka] peach (pl. *pesche*) [**pays**-kay]

pescanoce [pes-ka-**noh**-chay] nectarine.

pescatora, alla [pay-skah-**tore**-ah] with a fish or sea-food sauce.

pescatrice [pays-kah-**tree**-chay] monkfish, frogfish or angler fish, a fierce looking predator often used in soups; known as *rospo* in Venice and *boldro* in Tuscany.

Pesce di San Pietro [**pay**-shay dee san-**pyay**-troh] John Dory (fish).

pesce [**pay**-sahy] fish (pl. *pesci*); *pesce spada* is sword-fish; *pesci d'acqua dolce* are freshwater fish.

pesciolini [pesh-oh-**lee**-nee] tiny fish, small fry, e.g. white-bait.

pessichi [pes-**ee**-kee] peaches (Sicily).

pestariei [pas-tah-ree-**ay**-ee] little pasta pellets served with RICOTTA or other cheese.

pestazzule [pes-**tat**-soo-lay] Puglian pasta also known as PIZZELLE.

pesto [**pay**-stoh] a Ligurian sauce made by pulverising fresh basil and other ingredients with a pestle and mortar. The official list of ingredients given by the Consorzio del Pesto Genovese is as follows: fresh basil leaves, extra virgin olive oil, grated cheese (a mixture of PARMESAN and PECORINO), garlic, pine nuts or walnuts, coarse-grained salt. The resulting sauce is used with pasta and to flavour other dishes such as soup, doubling as a garnish or spread.

pesto modenese [**pay**-stoh moh-day-**nay**-zay] pork fat pounded with garlic and herbs, used as a spread, particularly in a CRESCENTINA, cut in half and filled with the *pesto*, or on *borlenghi* (see BORLENGO).

pesto rosso [**pay**-stoh **ross**-oh] Sicilian pesto, which uses less basil than the Genoese variety, substitutes pine nuts for almonds, and adds tomato.

pestun di fave [pay-**stoon** dee **fah**-vay] broad bean hash, made with cheese and garlic.

petali [**pay**-tal-ee] 'petals', delicate slivers.

Petit Rouge grape from Valle d'Aosta, used to make light, fruity red and rosé wines.

petronciana [pet-ron-**chah**-nah] a dialect word for aubergine.

petti see PETTO.

pettirossi [pet-ee-**ross**-ee] robins, small songbirds.

petto [**pet**-oh] (pl. *petti*), a breast; *petto di pollo* = chicken breast.

Pezzata [pet-**sah**-tah] a festival in Molise when quantities of barbecued lamb and mutton stew are consumed.

pezzetelli [pets-eh-**tell**-ee] small, cylindrical, indented chunks of pasta from Puglia, a kind of GNOCCHI.

pezzetti [pets-**ett**-ee] little pieces, morsels.

pezzogna [pay-**tzon**-ya] a type of sea bream, much prized in Campania.

piacentinu [pyatch-en-**teen**-oo] a pepper-and-saffron-infused, semi-hard cheese from Enna, Sicily. The name is derived from the Italian for 'pleasure': it is said that Roger II, king of Sicily in the early 12th century, had the cheese made in an attempt to cheer up his despondent wife. He instructed the cheese-makers to use saffron because of a widely-held belief in its uplifting qualities. Roger was married three times and had a number of mistresses. Which of these women was the intended recipient of the serotonin-rich cheese is unrecorded.

piada, piadina [pee-**ah**-dah, pyad-**ee**-nah] a type of flatbread, like a thick pancake, sometimes curled round a filling to make a kind of 'wrap' sandwich.

piastra, alla [**pyah**-strah] cooked on a griddle.

piatti freddi [pee-at-ee fred-ee] cold dishes.

piatto [pee-**at**-oh] 1. a dish, plate; 2. a course, e.g. *primo piatto* (first course); *piatto del giorno* (dish of the day).

piave [pee-**ah**-vay] a cow's milk cheese from the Veneto.

picagge [pick-**adge**-ay] Ligurian noodles, served with anchovy sauce, PESTO, etc.

piccante [pee-**kant**-ay] hot, piquant, spicy.

piccata [pee-**kaht**-ay] a slice or cutlet.

picchiettini [pick-yet-**ee**-nee] Umbrian pasta resembling matchsticks, traditionally served with tomato sauce or a meat RAGÙ.

piccione [pitch-**own**-ay] pigeon (pl. *piccioni*).

piccolo/a [**peek**-oh-loh] little.

pici [**pee**-chee] thick Tuscan noodles, typically made by hand.

piciocia [pitch-**otch**-ah] Sicilian chickpea POLENTA.

Picolit [**pee**-koh-lit] late-harvest and PASSITO dessert wine from Friuli-Venezia Giulia.

Piedirosso [pee-**ay**-dee **roh**-soh] red-wine grape grown in Campania, producing rich, bold wine.

Piedmont/Piemonte northwestern area of Italy, the heartland of the Risorgimento, the 19th-century movement for Italian unity, the first seat of Italy's monarchs, home of some of the country's heaviest industry, and birthplace of some of its finest cuisine. Much tourism to Piedmont is gastronomic: not only is the food excellent, but the region also produces some of Italy's finest wines, and many of its most enduring aperitifs and mixer drinks (Cinzano, Martini) were invented here. It was in Piedmont that the dry breadsticks known as GRISSINI were invented. The region is also internationally famous for its truffles, produced in the provinces of Alba and Mondovì. Of the excellent wines, the best known are BARBERA, BARBARESCO and BAROLO. This is a land of butter, not of olive oil. Cuisine is rich, with much emphasis on fine sausages, dairy produce, duck and goose.

Pigato [pee-**gah**-toh] a white grape from Liguria, producing young-drinking wines that pair well with seafood.

pignato grasso [pee-**nyah**-toh **gra**-soh] Neapolitan winter soup of pork and green leaf vegetables.

pignoccata, pignolata [peen-yoh-**kah**-tah, peen-yoh-**lah**-tah] a dessert similar to STRUFFOLI; sometimes coated in chocolate.

pignolate [peen-yoh-**laht**-ay] little balls of crushed almonds and pine nuts.

pignoli [**peen**-yoh-lee] see PINOLI.

pilotto [pee-**lot**-oh] in the Marche, a piece of lard used for basting. Dishes are described as *cotti* or *arrosti col pilotto*.

pimenta dioica [pee-**main**-tah dee-**oh**-ee-ca] allspice.

pimpinella [peem-pee-**nell**-ah] salad burnet, a wild plant sometimes used in salads: *non c'è insalata bella se non c'è la pimpinella* ('it's not a good salaid if it doesn't have *pimpinella*').

pincarelli see PENCARELLI.

pincinelli another name for PENCARELLI.

pinoli [pee-**no**-lee] pine nuts.

Pinot Grigio [pee-noh **gree**-joh] white-wine grape which produces a popular, easy-drinking wine. Its homeland is in the north, in Lombardy, Friuli-Venezia Giulia and Trentino.

Pinot Nero [pee-noh **nay**-roh] Italian name for Pinot Noir, the great red-wine grape of Burgundy. It Italy is it grown in the north and produces light, fruity wine.

pinzimonio [peent-see-**moan**-ee-oh] an ANTIPASTO of raw vegetables (crudités) and/or bread dressed with or dipped in a simple mix of olive oil and salt, with pepper, lemon juice or vinegar to taste.

piombi see ANCHELLINI.

pirciati [peer-**chat**-ee] pasta similar to BUCATINI.

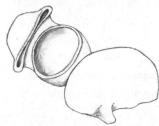

Pipe, pasta pipes.

pipe [**pee**-pay] short lengths of pasta shaped like bent tubes.

pisarei e fasò [pee-zah-**ray**-ee ay fah-**zoh**] GNOCCHI and BORLOTTI beans in an onion and tomato sauce (Emilia-Romagna).

pisci spata [**pish**-ee spat-ah] swordfish (Sicilian).

piscialandrea [peesha-lan-**dray**-ah] FOCACCIA with tomatoes and anchovies (Liguria). The name is said to derive from the great Genoese nobleman and sea captain Andrea Doria.

piselli [pee-**zell**-ee] peas; *pisellini* are *petits pois*, small or baby peas, received with great enthusiasm at the court of Louis XIV when they were first exported from Genoa to France in 1660.

pistacchio [pee-**stack**-yoh] pistachio.

pistingolo [pees-**teen**-goh-loh] a rich fruit cake from the Marche.

pitta in Catanzaro (Calabria), a thick bread ring, about 40cm across, tradition-ally served in sections with MURSEDDU or sliced to make a *murseddu* sandwich. Other-wise, the word can denote any kind of flatbread.

pitta 'mpigliata [**pee**-tah um-pee-**lyah**-tah] baked pastry rosettes filled with nuts, rai-sins, cinnamon, cloves, laced with a liqueur (e.g. STREGA) and drizzled with honey.

pizza [**peet**-zah] probably the most internationally famous dish of Italy: a flat, circular, leavened bread with a variety of toppings. It is a very ancient food (*see box opposite*). Pizzas come in two main forms: the thin, circular hand-tossed pizza of Naples, baked in a wood-fired oven; and Roman pizza, which has a thicker base and is cut into square portions. Deep pizzas with high outer walls, ideal for rich fillings and runnier sauces, are baked in pans rather than in the oven. Some of the most common types of pizza are listed overleaf.

A short digression on pizza

Pizza has existed in various forms since ancient times. In Book VII of the *Aeneid*, Virgil's epic poem recounting the founding of Rome, Aeneas and his men picnic on the Lazio shore after their voyage from Troy. They are so ravenous that they eat the circular flatbreads upon which their food was served. 'Heus! etiam mensas cosumimus?' cries Iulus: 'Oh no! Have we even eaten the plates?' It might be said that these flatbreads were the first true pizzas eaten on Italian soil.

The first reference to pizza by that name comes in the 10th century, in a document known as the *Codex Diplomaticus Caietanus*, from Gaeta, near the border of Lazio and Campania (the two regions that claim pizza as their own) where '*duodecim pizze*' (a dozen pizzas) are among many comestibles ordered for the Easter festivities. Over the centuries, Naples established itself as the most imaginative producer of *pizze*. The increasing popularity of tomatoes meant that by the mid-19th century pizzas were beginning to resemble the familiar product we know today. Finally in 1889, in honour of Margherita of Savoy, Queen of Italy, the Neapolitan pizza maker Raffaele Esposito created the first *tricolore*, a tomato, basil and cheese pizza celebrating the red, white and green flag of the newly unified Kingdom of Italy. Since then, the Margherita has become the simple template upon which all other pizzas are based.

Some common types of pizza

• *bianca*: 'white' pizza, without tomato; in Rome, pizza bread topped with olive oil, salt and rosemary sprigs;

• *capricciosa*: MOZZARELLA, tomato, mushrooms, artichokes, ham, olives, oil (in Rome, PROSCIUTTO and hard-boiled egg are added);

• *funghi e salsicce* (or *boscaiola*): MOZZARELLA, mushrooms and sausages, with or without tomato;

• *marinara*: tomato, garlic, oregano and olive oil;

• *Margherita*: tomato, MOZZARELLA, basil and olive oil;

• *Napoli*: in Rome, the name for a pizza topped with tomato, MOZZARELLA, anchovies and oil;

• *quattro formaggi*: four different cheeses, melted together or in decorative sectors;

• *quattro stagioni*: 'four seasons', with tomatoes, MOZZARELLA, mushrooms, ham, artichokes;

• *Romana*: the Neapolitan name for what the Romans call *Pizza Napoli*;

• *siciliana*: tomato, MOZZARELLA, capers, olive and anchovy.

pizza al formaggio [**peet**-zah al for-**madge**-oh] not a pizza, but a dome-shaped savoury loaf from the Marche, using several type of cheese.

pizzaiola [peets-eye-**oh**-lah] a tomato and garlic sauce.

pizzelle [peet-**zell**-ay] Puglian pasta similar to PACCOZZE but made without egg.

pizzoccheri [pits-**ock**-air-ee] buckwheat TAGLIATELLE served with potatoes, Swiss chard, butter and BITTO cheese.

platessa [pla-**tay**-sah] plaice.

polenta [pol-**ent**-ah] a maize flour hash prepared in one of two main ways: 1. as a savoury porridge topped with sauces, meat, fish, etc.; or 2. cur into squares and fried or grilled having first been allowed to cool and harden. This style is common in the Veneto. Regional polentas made of other flours (e.g chickpea) also exist.

polipo [**poll**-ee-poh] octopus.

pollame [poh-**lah**-may] poultry.

pollanca, pollastra, pollastrella [poh-**lan**-kah, poh-**las**-trah, poh-lah **strch**-lah] a young fattened hen.

pollo [**poh**-loh] chicken; strictly speaking a young hen which has not begun to lay; *pollo all diavola* is roast chicken with PEPERONCINO; *pollo in porchetta* is chicken stuffed with ham; *pollo novello* is spring chicken; *pollo rus-pante* is free-range chicken.

polpa [**pol**-pah] pulp, flesh.

polpetta [pol-**pay**-tah] (pl. *polpette*) a rissole; *polpette di carne* are meatballs.

polpettone [pol-pay-**toe**-nay] a meatloaf.

polpo [**pol**-poh] see POLIPO.

pomarola [pom-ah-**roh**-lah] *salsa pomarola*, tomato sauce.

pomo [**pom**-oh] apple.

pomodoro [pom-oh-**dor**-oh] tomato. *pomodori secchi*: dried tomatoes; *pomodorini:* cherry tomatoes; *pomodori perini:* plum tomatoes; *pomodori San Marzano* are a variety of plum tomato with DOP status, grown on the slopes of Mt Vesuvius.

How *pomodori* became safe to eat

The tomato was introduced to Europe in the 16th century as an ornamental plant, its seductive colour suggesting to many that it might be posionous. It was not until well into the late 17th century that cooks began to experiment with the food, encouraged by the activities of pet monkeys (there were many in the princely courts of Europe) who made no bones about seizing and eating the fruit and suffered no ill effects as a result. Today the tomato is a cornerstone of Italian gastronomy.

pompelmo [pom-**pail**-moh] grapefruit.

porceddu [por-chedh-**oo**] Sardinian roast suckling pig.

porcellana [por-chell-**ahn**-ah] purslane, a wild plant used for salads, also known as *portulaca*.

porcellino di latte [por-chell-**ee**-noh dee **lah**-tay] suckling pig. Also known as *porcello*.

porchetta [por-**ket**-ah] a whole young pig, boned and stuffed with herbs and roasted over an open fire or in a wood-burning oven; known in Sardinia as *porcetto* or *porceddu*.

porcinelli [por-cheen-**ell**-ee] brown and pink wild mushrooms; red boletus.

porcini [por-**cheen**-ee] *Boletus aedulis* (cepes); mushrooms. Dried *porcini*, along with other dried FUNGHI, are widely available.

porco [**pore**-koh] pig, also known as *maiale*.

porrata [poh-**rah**-tah] bacon and leek tart, a kind of quiche.

porro [**por**-roh] leek.

portafoglio [pore-tah-**foh**-lyoh] a dish where ingredients are placed in a 'portfolio', an outer wrapping, e.g. *portafogli di vitello alla salvia*: veal cutlets stuffed with sage.

portaluca SEE PORCELLANA.

Portoghese [por-toh-**gay**-zay] Portuguese.

pottaggio [pot-**aj**-oh] a thick soup or stew.

pranzo [**prant**-so] the midday meal; lunch.

prataioli [prat-eye-**ole**-ee] field mushrooms, meadow mushrooms; *Agaricus campestris*.

preboggion [pray-bodge-**on**] in Liguria, cooked herbs or greens.

presnitz [pray-**sneets**] a shortcrust pastry coil filled with dried fruits (Trieste).

prezzemolo [prets-**ay**-moh-loh] parsley.

prezzo fisso [**pray**-tsoh **fee**-soh] 'fixed price'; set menu.

prima colazione [**pree**-mah koh-lats-ee-**own**-ay] breakfast.

primi piatti [pree-mee **pyah**-tee] main courses.

Primitivo [pre-mee-**tee**-voh] red-wine grape introduced into Puglia in the 18th century, a cousin of the Californian Zinfandel, used to produce dark, intense wines.

primizie [pree-**meet**-see-ay] 'first fruits'; young vegetables.

propria [pro-pree-ah] own, e.g. *produzione propria*: local ('our own') produce.

prosciutto [pro-**shoo**-toh] ham; cured meat from the hind leg of a pig. There are two main types of *prosciutto*: *cotto* (cooked) and *crudo* (raw). All *prosciutto*, whether destined to be cooked or left raw, is first dried (the name *prosciutto* means 'dried out'). *Prosciutto cotto* is then usually deboned and steamed. *Prosciutto crudo*, raw ham that has been cured and air-dried, is what many people think of as typically Italian. The most famous type is *Prosciutto di Parma* ('Parma ham') but there are important regional variants, their flavour determined by factors such as the pigs' diet and the method and length of preparation. Another prized variety is *Prosciutto di San Daniele* from Friuli, which has lent its name to a popular restaurant chain, Pane Vino e San Daniele. *Prosciutto* is commonly eaten as an ANTIPASTO. *Prosciutto crudo* is also an important component of SALTIMBOCCA.

Prosecco [pro-**seck**-oh] a popular sparkling white wine made from grapes grown almost exclusively in the Veneto region.

provola [**pro**-voh-lah] fresh cow's milk PASTA FILATA cheese. Provola delle Madonie is a famous variety from the Madonie mountains of Sicily. In Campania they make a *provola* from buffalo milk.

provolone [pro-voh-**loh**-nay] firm, creamy cheese, a variant of PROVOLONE, mainly produced in the north of Italy, though a notable example from the south is *Provolone del*

Monaco, made from the milk of *Agerolese* cows, a breed from the Monti Lattari, the 'milky mountains', of Campania. Another is *Provolone Valpadana* from the Po basin.

prugna [**proon**-yah] plum (pl. *prugne*).

Prugnolo Gentile [**proon**-yo-loh jane-**tee**-lay] grape grown in the Montepulciano region of Italy, a clone of the SANGIOVESE Grosso. It is used to make Vino Nobile di Montepulciano.

puccia [**pooch**-ah] a bread roll (pl. *pucce*). *Puccia di Cortina* is a kind of FOCACCIA from Cortina d'Ampezzo, in the Veneto, made partly of rye flour and flavoured with ZIGOINR.

pucce e uliate [**pooch**-ay ay oo-lee-**ah**-tay] small bread. rolls (Puglia) made with black olives.

Puglia [**poo**-lyah] the fertile region in the heel of Italy. Puglia has always grown wheat, and this has made it historically wealthy. Its breads are excellent, as are its fruit and vegetables. Puglia also has 500 miles of coastline and a correspondingly varied and sophisticated fish cuisine. Puglia's wines, particularly those from the Salento peninsula, are becoming increasingly well known. Aleatico di Puglia is a wine dating back to the early 13th century, when it was first produced for the table of the Holy Roman Emperor Frederick II.

puina, puvina [**pwee**-nah] another name for RICOTTA.

puntarelle [poon-tah-**rell**-ay] wild chicory spears, eaten raw dressed with olive oil and anchovies. Typical of Rome.

punte d'ago [**poon**-tay **dah**-go] 'needle points', a pasta shape.

punte di asparagi [**poon**-tay dee as-**pah**-rah-jee] asparagus spears.

pupi di zucchero [**poop**-ee dee **tsoo**-kay-roh] painted festival dolls made of sugar (Sicily and the south), sometimes known as *pupi di cena*.

purea [poo-**ray**-ah] purée.

purpetti [poor-**pet**-ee] in Sicily, meatballs (*polpette*).

pussacaffè [poo-sah-kah-**feh**] see CAFFÈ.

puttanesca [poo-tan-**ay**-ska] a sauce for pasta of capers, black olives, garlic, olive oil, pepper, anchovies and tomatoes. The name derives from *puttana*, a whore. Theories abound as to origin: because it is quick to produce, some say it may derive from the fact that wayward wives, who had misbehaved all day rather than slaved at the stove, found it a swift way of providing their homecoming husbands with a good dinner.

puzzone di Moena [poo-**tsoh**-nay dee moe-**ay**-nah] famously smelly cheese from Trentino-Alto Adige.

quadrefiore [**kwod**-ray fee-**or**-ay] 'four flowers' PASTA CORTA shape.

quadrucci [kwod-**roo**-chee] pasta squares that are added to soups or broth.

quaglia [**kwa**-lyah] quail.

quaresimali [kwa-ray-zee-**mah**-lee] Lenten biscuits, made with almonds, sometimes in the form of alphabet letters coated in chocolate.

quartirolo [kwar-tee-**rohl**-oh] a soft, crumbly, agreeably sour cheese from Lombardy.

quasi crudo/a [**kwa**-zee **kroo**-doh] almost raw, very rare.

quattro formaggi [**kwat**-roh for-**madge**-ee] see PIZZA.

quattro stagioni [**kwat**-roh stadge-**own**-ee] see PIZZA.

quecciuolo see MURICE.

quinquinelle [queen-queen-**elle**-ay] fish dumplings, quenelles.

quinto quarto [**queen**-toh **kwar**-toh] the 'fifth quarter' of the animal: its entrails. A slaughtered animal is always divided into cuts graded by quality. When the choice bits have been sold, what remains is the so-called 'fifth' quarter: the offal, which in Rome in particular traditionally formed the staple food of the poor, who found (and still find) inventive ways of making it taste good. See PAJATA.

Radicchio di Treviso, the sought-after, bitter-tasting red endive from the Veneto region, with its slender, curling leaves.

rabarbaro [rah-**bahr**-bar-oh] rhubarb.

Raboso [rab-**oh**-zoh] a red-wine grape from the Veneto, high in tannin and acid.

racini [rah-**chee**-nee] grapes (Sicily).

radiatori [rah-dee-ah-**tore**-ee] pasta pieces resembling old-fashioned tubular radiators.

radicchio [rah-**dee**-kee-oh] not radish, which is *ravanello*, but endive or chicory. There are two main varieties the round-leafed *radicchio di Verona* and the long, curly-leafed *radicchio di Treviso*. The leaves are red, veined in white, and the taste is subtly bitter. It is a great delicacy of the Veneto region, often added to RISOTTO or cooked *alla* PIASTRA.

rafano [**rah**-fah-noh] horse-radish.

raffermo [ra-**fair**-mo] *pane raffermo* is stale bread, used to thicken soups and stews.

ragù [ra-**goo**] a thick, meat-based sauce, with onions, red wine and often tomatoes, slowly cooked and reduced. See also BOLOGNESE.

ramerino [ram-air-**ee**-noh] rosemary.

ramolaccio [ram-oh-**lah**-choh] radish.

rana, ranocchio [**rah**-nah, ran-**ock**-ee-oh] frog (pl. *rane*), the edible *Rana esculenta*. They abound in the wetlands of Lombardy and Piedmont and can be eaten whole, either deep fried or simmered with wine and herbs.

rana pescatrice [rah-nah pay-ska-**tree**-chay] the frog-fish or monkfish.

rapa [**rah**-pah] turnip. *Rape armate* ('turnips in armour') is a medieval dish that resurfaces from time to time. The 'armour' consists of a topping of cheese, butter and spices. The dish is ironically named, the point being that instead of protecting the turnips, the 'armour', the delicious cheesy carapace, renders them more vulnerable to assault (i.e. more appetising) than they might normally be.

rapa tedesca [rah-pah tay-**day**-skah] Jerusalem artichoke.

rapanello see RAVANELLO.

rape see RAPA.

raponzolo, raperonzo-lo [rap-**onts**-oh-loh, rap-air-**onts**-oh-loh] rampion, a vegetable with a parsnip-like root used in broth or served hot with cheese. The fairytale character Rapunzel is named after it.

Ratafià [rah-tah-fee-**ah**] a sweet cherry liqueur. Also known as *rattafia* [rat-**ah**-fee-ah]. It is sometimes used to flavour biscuits.

ravanello [rah-vah-**nell**-oh] radish (pl. *ravanelli*).

ravaggiolo, raveggiolo, raviggiolo [rah-**vah**-joh-loh] a fresh sheep or goat's cheese.

ravioli [rah-vee-**oh**-lee] PASTA RIPIENA, an ancient type and still one of the best known, both in Italy and beyond. Etymologists derive its name from *rape* ('turnips'), because early *ravioli* were typically filled with turnip greens. The earliest mention of

Ravioli, one of the most popular and best-known forms of pasta ripiena.

ravioli, in the 13th-century *Cronica* of the Franciscan friar Salimbene da Parma, does not mention this. In fact he describes eating a *'raviolus'* without a pastry casing. *Ravioli* today have their own official website (www.ravioli.it), which lists almost 30 recipes with fillings of meat, fish, vegetables and cheese. It also shows how square *ravioli* are made: not one by one, but from a single pasta sheet, dotted with blobs of filling, covered with a second sheet, and divided with a pastry cutter.

razza [**rats**-ah] 1. a skate or ray; *razza bianca* (white skate); *razza quattrocchi* ('four-eyed' skate), so-called because of its markings; 2. a breed or 'race', especially of cattle, e.g. *razza Agerolese*, a brown-coloured milking cow from Campania, whose milk is used for PROVOLONE; or the *razza Valdostana*, whose milk is used for REBLEC.

Razza Rendena [**rats**-ah ren-**day**-nah] 1. a cheese made from the milk of Rendena cows, native to the Val Rendena in Trentino. Rendena milk is also used for SPRESSA; 2. the cows themselves, also used as beef cattle.

reblec [reb-**leck**] fresh cow's milk cheese from the Valle d'Aosta.

Recioto [reh-**choh**-toh] Recioto from VALPOLICELLA is sweet red wine made from dried grapes in the same way as AMARONE, except that the wine does not ferment to dryness, thus containing some residual sugar. The sweet white Recioto di Soave is much rarer.

Refosco [re-**foss**-koh] red-wine grape grown in the Friuli-Venezia Giulia region, producing fully-flavoured, fruity wines.

regina [ray-**jee**-nah] carp.

regine [ray-**jee**-nay] literally 'queens', pasta named in honour of the House of Savoy, the royal family that supplied kings of Italy from Unification until the foundation of the modern republic in 1946; *reginelle* [ray-jee-**neh**-lay], 'little queens', are another Savoy pasta; *reginette* [ray-jee-**neh**-tay] are wavy-edged strips of pasta, the same as MAFALDE.

renga see ARINGA.

resentin [ray-sayn-**teen**] see CAFFÈ.

rete [ray-tay] literally a 'net'; caul, a fatty membrane. See OMENTO.

rhum [hrr-**oom**] rum.

ribes [ree-bays] redcurrants.

Ribolla Gialla [ree-**boll**-ah **jall**-ah] a white-wine grape cultivated in Friuli.

ribollita [ree-boll-**ee**-tah] bean and vegetable stew of Tuscan origin. The soup is made a day in advance and is then reboiled (*ribollita*) to intensify and mature the flavour. Red cabbage, kale and stale bread are the main ingredients and there are variations on the theme throughout the region.

Ricasoli, Baron Bettino [ree-**kah**-zoh-lee] (1809–80) second Prime Minister of united Italy and a native Tuscan, credited with drawing up the first official 'recipe' for the CHIANTI blend.

ricci [ree-chee] see RICCIO.

ricci di donna [**ree**-chee- dee **donn**-ah] 'a woman's curls', a type of pasta.

ricciarelli [reech-ah-**rell**-ee] deliacte honey and almond biscuits from Siena, Tuscany.

riccio di mare [**reech**-oh dee **mah**-ray] sea urchin (pl. *ricci*).

riccioli Amalfitani [reech-oh-li a-mal-fi-**tahn**-ee] little curl-shaped pieces of pasta.

ricciolina [rich-oh-**lee**-nah] *torta ricciolina* is a kind of marzipan tart.

ricotta [rick-**oht**-ah] a soft cheese made from whey, the name meaning literally 'recooked", alluding to the manufacturing process. Standard cheese is made from milk by extracting the curds. To make *ricotta*, the leftover whey is heated, resulting in a runny, protein-rich and highly versatile cheese, ideal for

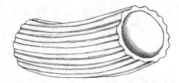

Rigatoni, ridged, tubular pasta used in Rome as a vehicle for *pajata*.

adding to sauces. There are many regional variants, using milk from cows, sheep, buffalo and goats, and including smoked *ricottas* and *ricotta salata*, a *ricotta* preserved with salt and then left to age and harden in just the same way as a conventional PECORINO.

rigaglie [ree-**gah**-lyay] offal from poultry.

rigate, rigati [ree-**gah**-tay, ree-**gah**-tee] of pasta, ridged.

rigatoni [ree-gah-**toh**-nee] pasta in the form of short, ridged tubes.

rinforzo, insalata di [een-sah-**lah**-tah dee reen-**forts**-soh] a salad of cauliflower, anchovies, olives and pickled peppers served in Naples over Christmas and Epiphany.

rinfresco [reen-**frays**-koh] refreshment (pl. *rinfreschi*).

Ripasso [ree-**pah**-so] type of VALPOLICELLA made by a second fermentation of a non-SUPERIORE wine on used RECIOTO skins.

ripieno/a [ree-pee-ay-**ay**-noh] stuffed or filled.

riserva [ree-**zair**-vah] reserve: a high-quality version of a wine, often with a greater alcoholic content, aged for longer.

risi e bisi [**ree**-zee ay **bee**-zee] rice with young peas, a speciality of the Veneto.

riso [ree-zoh] rice.

risotto [ree-**zott**-oh] rice simmered slowly in stock (*brodo*) until the liquid has been absorbed. ARBORIO rice is widely held to be the best for *risotto*, capable of absorbing the various attributes of the other ingredients—stock, wine, butter, olive oil—without losing its own texture and flavour. Perhaps the most famous of all *risotti* is *risotto alla milanese* (flavoured with saffron). Its home is certainly the north of Italy, where rice is grown. Delicious truffle *risotti* are also common, and in the Veneto they make *risotto* with RADICCHIO. *Risotto* is not the same as *riso in brodo* ('rice in broth'), in which rice is one of several ingredients in a runny soup.

ristretto see CAFFÈ.

robiola [roh-bee-**oh**-lah] a soft, creamy cheese from Piedmont, made from sheep's, cow's or goat's milk, popular as a basis for sauces.

roccocò [rock-ock-**oh**] a Neapolitan ring-shaped Christmas biscuit.

rognoni, rognoncini [ron-**yoan**-ee, ron-yon-**chee**-nee] kidneys. *Rognoncini trifolati* are sliced and braised in wine.

Romagna see EMILIA-ROMAGNA.

romanesco [rom-ah-**nay**-skoh] green or yellow-green broccoli with tightly-packed, pointed florets.

rombo [**rom**-boh] turbot or brill.

Rosa Camuna [**roh**-zah ka-**moo**-nah] a mild cheese from Val Camonica, Lombardy.

rosato [roh-**zah**-toh] rosé.

rosetta [roh-**zett**-ah] see MICHETTA.

rosmarino [ross-mah-**ree**-noh] rosemary.

Rosolio [roe-**zohl**-ee-oh] a liqueur of distilled rose petals, used as a mixer drink.

rospo [**ross**-poh] frogfish, monkfish or angler fish.

rossi leggeri [**ross**-ee-ledge-**air**-ee] light red wines.

rosso [**ross**-oh] 1. red. *In rosso* means cooked with tomatoes; 2. *rosso d'uovo*: egg yolk.

roticciana [ros-tee-**chah**-nah] grilled spare ribs.

rotini [roe-**teen**-ee] corkscrew-shaped pasta.

rotolo [**roh**-toh-loh] a swiss roll; a roly poly.

rrau see RAGÙ.

ruccolo, ruccul [rook-oh-loh, rook-**ool**] 1. a kind of flatbread; 2. bread filled with chunks of ham and sausage.

Ruchè [roo-**keh**] Piedmontese red-wine grape.

Rucola, a pungent and popular salad leaf.

rucola, rughetta, ruchetta [**roo**-koh-lah, roog-**ett**-ah, rook-**ett**-ah] rocket or arugula, a pleasantly peppery-tasting salad vegetable. It has been popular in Italy since Roman times, when it was thought to have aphrodisiac properties (it was often grown near statues of the fertility god, Priapus). Today it is found not only in salads but in pasta sauces and rice dishes.

ruote [roo-**oh**-tay] wheel-shaped pasta.

ruspante [roos-**pant**-ay] free-range (chicken).

russuliddu [roo-soo-lidh-**oo**] in Sicily, fried red mullet.

rustica, alla [**roo**-stee-kah] 'country' style.

ruta [**roo**-tah] rue.

saba, sapa [**sah**-bah, **sah**-pah] grape must.

sa fregula [sa **fray**-goo-lah] pasta balls, couscous.

sagne chine [**sahn**-yay **keen**-ay] a rich Calabrian lasagne where the pasta is interleaved with a stuffing of meatballs, artichokes, mushrooms, herbs, PECORINO and egg.

sagne a pezze [**sahn**-yay-ah-**pet**-zay] a lozenge-shaped flat pasta from Molise, also known as *tacconelle*.

sagnozze [san-**yots**-ay] in Lazio and the Abruzzo, a thick PASTA LUNGA.

sagra [**sag**-rah] a festival, often celebrating the food or wine of a town, region or province.

Sagrantino [sah-gran-**tee**-noh] red-wine grape from Umbria, much prized and often blended with SANGIO-VESE to make ink-dark, fruity wines that age very well, e.g. Sagrantino di Montefalco, a DOCG wine made from 100 percent Sagrantino.

salama da sugo [sa-**lah**-mah da **soo**-goh] a kind of Ferrarese haggis, consisting of pork neck, belly, throat, liver and tongue salted and seasoned, mixed with unpasteurised red wine and packed into a stout pig's bladder.

salame and **salume** [sal-ah-may, sal-**oo**-may] cured meats (*see box below* and also see SPECK, PROSCIUTTO, BRESAOLA, etc).

salami *see box below*.

Salume, *salame* and salami

In Britain and the USA *salami* is the accepted term to denote the distinctive cured sausages, sold whole or in slices in delicatessens and supermarkets or served in sandwiches and as *hors d'oeuvres*. The usage is incorrect, albeit harmlessly so, since *salami* is the plural of *salame*.

Both *salame* and *salume* are derived from the Latin word *sal*, meaning salt, the main ingredient in the curing process. But while *salume* is the general term for all cured, cold meats, a *salame* is just one example. A *salame* tends to be made of cheaper, leftover bits of meat, which is salted, seasoned and cured uncooked. Some *salume* are called *insaccati* ('en-sacked', because they are stuffed into intestines to keep their shape). Important subgroups of these are *salsiccie* (roughly the equivalent of the English 'sausages') and *soppressate* (from the verb 'to crush'). Many kinds of meat are used in *salume*, though by far the most common is pork. A *salumeria* is a shop specialising in cured meats and sausage.

---

salamoia [sal-ah-**moy**-ah] brine.

salamora [sal-ah-**mor**-ah] a marinade, made by steeping herbs and spices in oil. Many recipes exist, depending on what kind of meat or fish the marinade is intended for.

salatino [sal-ah-**teen**-oh] a savoury snack, an appetiser.

salato/a [sa-**lah**-toh] 1. sa-voury, the opposite of *dolce*; 2. salted, salty.

sale [**sah**-lay] salt.

salicornia [sal-ee-**korn**-ee-ah] succulent maritime plant, known as sea asparagus. It is a popular accompaniment to fish dishes, sometimes pickled.

salignoun [sal-een-**yoon**] a RICOTTA from the Valle d'Aosta, flavoured with herbs and PEPERONCINO.

salimora SEE SALAMORA.

salmì, in [sal-**mee**] a way of cooking game involving lengthy stewing in wine with herbs and seasoning. *Lepre in salmì* is jugged hare.

salmone [sal-**moan**-ay] salmon.

salmorigano SEE SALMORIGLIO.

salmoriglio [sal-mor-**eel**-yo] a sauce made of olive oil, lemon juice, garlic, salt, parsley and oregano. It can be eaten hot or cold or used as a fish marinade. It is also known as *salmorigano*.

salsa [**sal**-sah] sauce. See also VERDE.

salsiccia [sal-**seetch**-ah] a sausage, an INSACCATO made of raw seasoned meat stuffed into an intestine. They can be eaten hot or cold, but must be cooked first. *Salsicce* differ widely from region to region.

salsicciotto [sal-see-**chot**-oh] a large banger or frankfurter.

saltato/a [sal-**tah**-toh] sau-téed.

saltimbocca [sal-teem-**bock**-ah] a Roman speciality, veal cutlets topped with PRO-SCIUTTO and simmered in white wine and butter with sage. The name means 'jump in the mouth', alluding to the irresistible taste of the dish.

salume SEE SALAME.

salvia [**sal**-vee-ah] sage.

sambuca [sam-**boo**-kah] an anise-flavoured DIGESTIVO often served with coffee beans set alight on its surface, which set off an incandescent blue glow.

sambuco [sam-**boo**-koh] elderberry.

sambusaj [sam-boo-**sadge**] in

Piedmont a triangular pasta, like RAVIOLI, stuffed with spiced meat and also reminiscent of the *samosa*. The name derives from the Arabic *sambusak*.

sammirighiu [sammy-**rig**-you] Sicilian for SALMORIGLIO.

Sampiero [sam-**pyay**-roh] John Dory.

sanato [sa-**nah**-toh] young, milk-fed veal from Piedmont.

sanbudello [san-boo-**dell**-oh] a coarse SALAME from Arezzo, Tuscany.

Sangiovese [san-joe-**vay**-zay] red-wine grape used to produce the fine wines of Tuscany such as CHIANTI CLASSICO, and BRUNELLO di Montalcino (Brunello is a clone of Sangiovese Grosso). The principal grape in all Chianti wines, Sangiovese is intense in colour and high in acidity.

sangue [**san**-gway] blood. *Al sangue* = rare.

sanguinaccio [san-gwee-**natch**-yoh] 1. a blood sausage; 2. a chocolate dessert.

sanguinello [san-gwee-**nell**-oh] blood orange.

santoreggia [san-toh-**redge**-yah] savory (herb).

Saonara [sah-oh-**nah**-rah] a town in the province of Padua in the Veneto known for its horsemeat. Some say the tradition of eating horsemeat in the Veneto dates back to the early trade routes from Genoa and other cities to Venice. Many horses were too broken down to make the return journey and were therefore slaughtered and eaten. The slaughter of horses is a contentious subject today. Enjoy *prosciutto di cavallo* while you can...

saor [sah-**oar**] a marinade of onions, sage and white wine typical of the Veneto, where it is used with sardines.

sapa [**sah**-pah] grape must.

sapore [sap-**ore**-ay] flavour, taste.

saracinesca [sar-ah-chee-**nay**-skah] sauce made of almonds, raisins, ginger, cinnamon, cloves and black pepper. It imparts a distinct Middle-Eastern ('Saracen') flavour to certain Venetian dishes.

sarago fasciato [sah-rah-go fash-**ah**-toh] the two-banded sea bream.

sarda [sahr-dah] a pilchard, sardine; *sardina*: a young pilchard, i.e. a sardine.

sardenaira, sardenara, sardinara [sar-den-**aï**-rah, sar-den-**ah**-rah, sar-dee-**nah**-rah] a Ligurian FOCACCIA with a topping of tomato, capers and anchovies. It is also known as *Pizza all'Andrea* or PISCIAL-ANDREA.

Sardinia Though the island is named after the sardine, Sardinia is not famed for its fish dishes. Pirate raids historically forced the population inland, the most traditional dishes focus instead on lamb, rabbit, game and sheep's cheese. Myrtle is commonly used as a flavouring, notably in the famous roast suckling pig. One maritime ingredient that is still prevalent is BOTTARGA, the 'Sicilian caviar'.

The CANNONAU red wine is said to be unusually rich in antioxidants.

sartù [sar-**too**] the *sartù di riso* [dee **ree**-zoh] or *sartù napoletano* [nah-poh-lay-**tah**-noh] is a Neapolitan baked rice pie, filled with meatballs, sausage, cheese, mushrooms and peas (though recipes vary) .

Sassicaia [sa-see-**keye**-ah] all-Cabernet SUPERTUSCAN from the BOLGHERI region.

sasizza [sah-**seets**-ah] in Sicily, a sausage.

sas alisanzas SEE ALISANZAS.

sa taccula SEE TACCULA.

savoiardi [sah-voy-**ahr**-dee] sponge fingers.

savor SEE SAOR.

sbombata [sbom-**bah**-tah] Umbrian pasta dish in which a sheet of pasta is placed in a baking tray that is subsequently filled with a sauce of giblets, tomatoes, celery and carrots layered with more pasta sheets before being baked.

sbriciolata, sbriciolona,

sbrisolona [sbreech-oh-**lah**-tah, sbreech-oh-**loan**-ah, sbree-zoh-**loan**-ah] 1. a sweet crumbly cake from Lombardy and the north; 2. *sbriciolata* (masc. *sbriciolato*) means 'crumbled'.

sbrofadej [sbroff-ah-**day**] pasta from Lombardy resembling stout VERMICELLI, made with egg, flour and grated nutmeg, served in broth.

scabeggio [ska-**bedge**-oh] fried fish marinated in garlic, lemon juice and sage (vinegar and white wine may also be added). The dish is typical of Moneglia in Liguria. The word shares a root with the Spanish *escabeche*, also a sour marinade.

scaldatelli [skal-dah-**tell**-ee] ring-shaped bread rolls flavoured with fennel seeds, cooked in boiling water and then baked in the oven until golden brown (Puglia).

scalille [ska-**leel**-ay] pastry knots fried and then glazed in syrup of figs (Calabria).

scallopino [skal-oh-**pee**-noh] an escalope, a thin, pounded piece of meat, commonly veal (pl. *scallopini*).

scalogna [ska-**loan**-yah] scallion, shallot.

scamone [ska-**moan**-ay] rump (of beef).

scamorza [skam-**orts**-sah] stringy PASTA FILATA-type cow's milk cheese from Abruzzo, Molise, Campania and Puglia.

scampi [**skam**-pee] the Italian name for Norway lobsters, langoustines, Dublin Bay prawns.

scapece [ska-**pay**-chay] a method of pickling fish or vegetables. See SCABEGGIO.

scarcedda [skar-**chedd**-ah] Easter cakes from Puglia and Basilicata. Both sweet and savoury versions exist; the sweet type are often iced.

scarola [ska-**role**-ay] escarole, broad-leaved endive.

scarpazza [skar-**pats**-ah] a vegetable tart, also known as *stirpada* and *scherpada*.

scarpinocc [skar-pee-**nock**] cheese-filled pasta from Lombardy.

scarteddate [skar-ted-**ah**-tay] fried Christmas biscuits in southern Italy. A version of CARTELLATE.

scelta [**shell**-tah] choice, e.g. *contorno a scelta*, a choice of vegetables.

scherpada see SCARPAZZA.

schiacciata [skee-atch-**ah**-tah] a thin Tuscan flatbread, usually topped with olive oil and salt.

schiacciato/a [skee-atch-**ah**-toh] crushed, mashed.

schiaffoni [skyaff-**oh**-ee] see PACCHERI.

schie [skee-**ay**] small grey shrimp of the Venetian lagoon, eaten whole in RISOTTO.

schienale [skee-ay-**nah**-lay] bone marrow from the spine.

Schioppettino [ski-op-ett-**een**-oh] dark red Friulan grape, used for eating and to make fruity red wines.

schiuma [skee-**oo**-mah] froth, foam.

schlutzer tirolesi [**shloot**-ser tee-roh-**lay**-zee] spinach and ricotta-filled RAVIOLI from Trentino-Alto Adige.

scialatielli [shah-lat-**yell**-ee] square-section noodles from Campania, typical of the Amalfi Coast, somewhat resembling short TAGLIATELLE. They are often served with seafood sauces.

sciarrano [sha-**rah**-no] the saltwater perch.

sciatt [shatt] buckwheat pancake with cheese and GRAPPA (Lombardy).

scipelle 'mbusse [shee-**pell**-ay um-**boo**-say] cheese-filled crêpes in broth.

sciroppo [shee-**rop**-oh] syrup.

sciule piene [**shoo**-lay pee-**ay**-nay] Piedmontese stuffed onions. Stuffing recipes vary: some use raisins, while others call for meat and cheese. The stuffing is thickened with bread soaked in milk.

sconciglio see MURICE.

scorfano [skor-**fah**-noh] scorpion fish. There is more than one type: *scorfano rosso* (red), *scorfano nero* (black) and the *scorfanotto* (a mottled variety). They are a staple of fish stews and can also be eaten roasted or grilled.

scorzato/a [scorts-**ah**-toh] peeled.

scorza [**skorts**-ah] the peel (of a fruit or vegetable), or rind (of a cheese). *Scorza candita* is candied peel. *Scorze d'arance candite* are candied orange peels.

scorzonera [scorts-on-**ay**-rah] a type of salsify, a plant prized for its edible root, which is cooked in the same way as a parsnip.

scottato/a [skoh-**tah**-toh] blanched, parboiled.

scremato [scray-**mah**-toh] skimmed (milk).

scucuzzu [skoo-**koots**-oo] a type of pasta from Liguria.

scungilli [skoon **jill**-ee] whelks, served sautéed in sauce, often spicy.

scuro/a [**skoo**-roh] dark.

seadas, seattas, sebadas [say-**ah**-das, say-**att**-as, say-**bah**-das] Sardinian RAVIOLI, large, round and sweet, filled with cheese and grated lemon, and served fried and drizzled with honey.

secale see SEGALE.

secco/a [**seck**-oh] dry, dried (pl. *secchi, secche*).

sedanini rigati [say-dan-**nee**-nee ree-**gaht**-ee] pasta in the form of small celery stalks, i.e. ribbed and grooved in the same way as the plant.

sedano [say-**dan**-oh] celery.

segale [**say**-gah-lay] rye, a kind of grass that has been cultivated since ancient times in northern Italy, where the climate and terrain is unfriendly to wheat. It is prized for its grain, which is suitable both for human consumption and for animal feed. Today, many regional breads and pastas are made from a mixture of wheat and rye flour. Recent Swiss research has shown that bread made from *segale bianca*, the kernel of the rye grain, acts as an excellent natural insulin regulator and can therefore help those at risk from diabetes. Many breads are made from a mixture of wheat flour and rye bran, which does not

Above: *seppia*, a cuttlefish, fatter in the body than the *calamari*, or squid (pictured opposite).

have the same beneficial effect.

sella [**sell**-ah] saddle, e.g. *sella d'agnello*: saddle of lamb.

selvaggina [sell-vah-**jee**-nah] game.

semelle [say-**mell**-ay] round bread rolls with a cleft in the middle (Florence). The name derives from the German *Semmel* and dates from the period of Austrian rule in Tuscany.

semi [**say**-mee] seeds.

semifreddo [**say**-mee **fred**-oh] literally 'half cold', a dessert made of ice cream and sponge cake.

semola battuta [**say**-moh-lah bah-**too**-tah] irregular little lumps of pasta cooked in broth (Puglia).

semolina [say-mo-**lee**-nah] a flour ground from durum wheat, widely used to make pasta dough. See FARINA.

semplice [**same**-plee-chay] simple.

senape [**say**-nap-ay] mustard.

senza [**sent**-sah] without.

seppia [**sepp**-yah] cuttlefish. There are several types, of which *seppietta* and *seppiola* are two. Styles of cooking do not differ: the flesh is either grilled, fried or stewed, and is also eaten cold in salads. *Seppioline* are very small cuttlefish; *uova di seppia* is cuttlefish roe. *Nero di seppia* is the ink, used to colour and flavour GNOCCHI, pasta and RISOTTO. *Seppia* is similar to, but not the same as, squid (CALAMARI).

seras [**say**-ras] tangy cheese from the Valle d'Aosta.

serpentone [sair-pain-**tone**-ay] coiled or spiral-shaped pastry from Umbria and Lazio, made of ground almonds. Also known as *torciglione*.

serviti con contorno [sair-**vee**-tee con kon-**torn**-oh] served with vegetables (meaning you do not need to order these separately).

servizio compreso [sair-**veets**-yo com-**pray**-zoh] service charge included.

sesamo [**say**-zam-oh] sesame.

sevadas SEE SEADAS.

sfarricciato [sfar-ee-**chaht**-oh] blood pudding (Molise).

sfoglia matta [**sfoll**-ya **mat**-ah] lit. 'crazy pastry', a term for puff pastry or *pasta sfoglia*.

sfogliatella [sfoll-ya-**tell**-ah] Neapolitan dessert: a ruffled pastry shaped like a scallop shell, filled with RICOTTA or custard (pl. *sfogliatelle*).

sfoglio, sfogghiu [**sfoh**-lyoh, **sfog**-yoo] a puff pastry pie (Sicily).

sformato [sfor-**mah**-toh] a vegetable flan or soufflé.

sfuso [**sfoo**-zoh] *vino sfuso* is loose wine.

sgabei [sgab-**ay**-ee] strips of fried bread dough, eaten either plain or with a ham or cheese filling.

sgombro [**sgom**-broh] mackerel.

sgroppino [sgro-**pee**-noh] the Italian equivalent of a coupe colonel: a DIGESTIVO or palate cleanser between courses consisting of lemon sorbet laced with vodka. Popular in the Veneto.

sguazzabarbuz SEE MALTAGLIATI.

sgusciato/a [sgoosh-**ah**-toh] shelled, e.g. of nuts (pl. *sgusciati, sgusciate*).

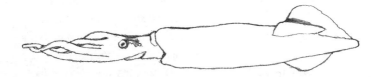

siccioli see CICCIOLI.

Sicily the large island at the toe of Italy, with a very varied gastronomic tradition reflecting its geographical position and complex history. The soil is fertile and the climate good, meaning that bread, fruit, vegetables and meat are all excellent. Sicilians eat a lot of fish, and their confectionery is second to none, thanks in part to the introduction of sugar cane by the Arabs and chocolate by the Spanish. Sicily also produces abundant wine: according to legend, vines first grew here on the slopes of Etna, springing up under the feet of Dionysus.

sidro [see-droh] cider.

siliquastro [silly-kwas-troh] 1. the Judas tree. Its flowers (*fiori di siliquastro*) are sometimes seen on recherché menus; 2. siliquastrum was the medieval name for PEPERONCINO.

Silter [silt-uh] a mild cow's cheese made in the lower Val Camonica, Lombardy.

simenza e calia [see-ment-sah eh kahl-yah] on feast days in Sicily street stalls sell roasted chickpeas (*calia*) and pumpkin seeds coated in sugar (*simenza*).

sindria [seen-dree-ah] watermelon (Sardinia).

slattato [slat-ah-toh] soft, fresh cow's milk cheese from the Marche.

Slow Food A movement inspired by an organisation called Arcigola, founded in 1986 as a protest against the proposed opening of a branch of McDonald's near the Spanish Steps in Rome. There is now an international network of towns and villages that subscribe to the Slow ethic: residents are encouraged to cook and eat in a leisurely way, using local produce and respecting local traditions. Slow Food also publishes restaurant and wine guides.

smacafam [smack-ah-fam] the 'hunger-beater', potato polenta baked with cream and SALAME (Trentino-Alto Adige).

smitane [**smee**-tah-nay] a sauce made of onion, cream or sour cream and wine. It goes well with game birds.

Soave [so-**ah**-vay] dry white wine from the Verona area of the Veneto, mainly made from the Garganega grape.

sodo [**so**-doh] of an egg, hard-boiled: *uovo sodo* (pl. *uova sodi* or *sode*).

soffritto [soff-**ree**-toh] a combination of celery, onion and carrot lightly fried in olive oil, the foundation of many Italian recipes. Garlic, parsley, fresh sage and other herbs may be added to taste.

sogliola [**sohl**-yoh-lah] sole. *Alla mugnaia* = meunière

Solaia [so-**leye**-ah] like TIG-NANELLO, a wine from the Chianti region that is made from Bordeaux grape varieties and does not label itself a Chianti. It is one of the so-called SU-PERTUSCANS.

soppressata [sop-res-**ah**-tah] lit. 'crushed' or 'squashed', a kind of SALUME, a sausage packed into an animal's intestine, often (but not always) soft and suitable for spreading.

sorbetto [sor-**bet**-oh] a sorbet. The word derives from sherbet, a cold drink introduced to Sicily by the Arabs and consisting of water and fruit pulp sweetened with sugar. An *aria di sorbetto,* the 'sorbet aria', was a convention in 19th-century Italian opera, a song performed by one of the minor singers during which ice cream vendors would circulate through the theatre. A *sorbetto* is finer-grained than a GRANITA.

sorcetti [sore-**chet**-ee] a type of GNOCCHI typical of the Abruzzo, often made with spinach.

s'oriattu [sorry-**at**-tu] Sardinian barley bread.

sospiri [sos-**pee**-ree] 'sighs', little sweetmeats that can take a wide variety of forms, from biscuits to fairy cakes.

sottaceti [sot-ah-**chay**-tee] pickles (lit. 'under vinegar').

sotto [**sot**-oh] in, on or under,

e.g. *tonno sott'olio*: tuna in oil.

spadellato [spah-dell-**ah**-toh] sautéed.

spaghetti [spag-**ett**-ee] literally, 'small strings', the most famous Italian pasta.

spaghettoni [spag-ett-**own**-ay] extra thick, long spaghetti.

On the origins of spaghetti

Patriotic Italians keen to refute claims that spaghetti was introduced to Italy from China by Marco Polo in the late 13th century seize with glee on the *Tabula Rogeriana*, a book of maps with accompanying commentary commissioned c. 1140 from the Arab cartographer Muhammad al-Idrisi by King Roger II of Sicily. In that book, al-Idrisi refers to the Sicilian town of Trabia, where 'an abundance of water turns numerous mills, where they grind flour used to make *itryah*, a particular type of pasta made up of exceedingly long strings...'. The word *itryah* survives today in Italianised form, as *tria*, a kind of long pasta still eaten in the south. Marco Polo may well have brought a similar food from China to the Veneto. But wheat-growing Sicily and Puglia were already enjoying spaghetti before he was even born.

---

spagnolo [**span**-yo-lo] Spanish.

spalla [**spa**-lah] shoulder of veal, lamb or pork. *Spalla di San Secondo* is a cooked ham from Emilia-Romagna.

spalmare [spal-**mah**-ray] to spread; *spalmabile* [spal-**mah**-bee-lay] = spreadable.

sparacanaci [spa-rah-kan-**atch**-ee] in Sicily, fried baby mullet.

spätzli [**shpets**-lee] *gnocchetti* from Trentino-Alto Adige.

specchio [**speck**-yoh] literally, a mirror. On menus a *specchio* is an accompaniment designed to reflect or enhance the principal ingredient, e.g. *zucchini ripieni* (stuffed courgettes) *su specchio di* (on a 'mirror' of) *pomodoro fresco* (fresh tomato).

speck [shpeck] juniper-flavoured ham, widely made in Trentino-Alto Adige and northern Italy.

spezie [**spets**-yay] spices.

spezzatino [spets-ah-**teen**-oh] meat stew.

spianata [spya-**nah**-tah] a kind of FOCACCIA, often strewn with rosemary.

spicchio [**speek**-yoh] (pl. *spicchi*) a piece, a segment. *Uno spicchio d'aglio* = a clove of garlic.

spiedini [spee-ay-**dee**-nee] anything grilled or roasted on skewers (*spiedi*); kebabs.

spiedo [spee-**ay**-doh] a spit for roasting.

spiga [**spee**-gah] an ear (of wheat, corn).

spighe [**spee**-gay] pasta shaped like ears of wheat.

spigola [**spee**-go-lah] a type of sea bass. *Persico spigola* is striped bass.

spina [**spee**-nah] 1. a spine or thorn; 2. a tube, hence *birra alla spina*, draught beer.

spinaci [spee-**natch**-ee] spinach (always plural), a popular vegetable served as a side dish, mixed with pasta dough to make green pasta, or used as a pasta stuffing.

spinatspätzle [shpee-naht-shpets-lee] spinach *gnocchetti* from Trentino-Alto Adige.

spirali [spee-**rah**-lee] spiral pasta.

spongata [spong-**gah**-tah] a Christmas pie with a short-crust pastry exterior and a filling of nuts and dried fruit.

spratti [**sprah**-tee] sprats.

spremuta [spray-**moo**-tah] freshly squeezed fruit juice.

spressa [**spray**-sah] a cow's milk cheese from Trentino-Alto Adige.

sproccolati [sprock-oh-**lah**-tee] dried figs filled with fennel seeds.

spruzzamusi 'snout-sprayers', a regional name for pasta served in a sloppy sauce.

spugnole [**spoon**-yo-lay]

morel mushrooms.

spumante [spoo-**man**-tay] sparkling, of wine.

spumone [spoo-**moan**-ay] a general term for light, fluffy desserts, egg-meringues or mousses (pl. *spumoni*).

spuntini [spoon-**teen**-ee] snacks.

squacquero, squacquerone [skwak-**way**-roh, skwak-way-**roan**-ay] very soft, almost runny cow's milk cheese from Emilia-Romagna.

squaliato/a [skwal-**ya**-toh] melted.

squalo [**skwah**-loh] shark.

stagionato [stadge-on-**ah**-toh] lit. 'seasoned'; of cheese, aged or matured.

stagione [stadge-**own**-ay] season, e.g. *verdure di stagione*: seasonal vegetables; *fuori stagione*: out of season.

stambecco [stam-**beck**-oh] the wild mountain goat of Valle d'Aosta and the alpine regions.

stecca di cioccolato [steck-ah dee chock-oh-**lat**-oh] chocolate bar.

stecchi alla genovese [steck-ee alla jain-oh-**vay**-zee] wooden skewers stuck with chicken, chicken liver and mushrooms dipped in béchamel sauce, breaded and fried.

stelline [stell-**ee**-nay] tiny stars, a pasta shape, also known as *stellette, stellettine, stelle, astri, fiori di sambuco*.

STG *Specialità Tradizionale Garantita*, official appellation awarding 'traditional' status to certain products to protect them from imitations.

stigghiola [stig-**yo**-lah] lamb's intestines, traditionally wound around a leek, and then cooked on a brazier. A dish from Sicily, where it is sold as street food.

stile [**stee**-lay] style.

stirpada see SCARPAZZA.

stoccafisso [stock-ah-**fee**-soh] cod or other white fish that has been dried and preserved without the use of salt (compare BACCALÀ, which is salt cod). Both *baccalà* and *stoccafisso* are thoroughly soaked in water before being use.

storione [stoh-ree-**own**-ay] sturgeon.

stracchino [strack-**ee**-noh] Lombard cow's milk cheese with a soft, creamy texture. See CRESCENZA.

stracciamus [stratch-ah-**moos**] see SPRUZZAMUSI.

stracciatella [strah-cha-**teh**-lah] 1. broth made by adding beaten eggs and PARMESAN cheese to stock; 2. *fior di latte* ice cream (see GELATO) with chocolate chips.

strachin [strah-**keen**] see STRACCHINO.

stracotto [strah-**kot**-oh] 1. a stew, often of beef in red wine; 2. overcooked, the opposite of *al dente*.

straffatto [strah-**fah**-toh] over-ripe, of fruit.

strangolapreti [stran-go-lah-**pray**-tee] 'priest choker', an example of anti-clerical gastroterminology. 1. a potato GNOCCHI, sometimes made with spinach. The idea is that a greedy priest, while gorging himself, might get one stuck in his throat and choke; 2. In

some parts of Italy the term is a synonym for STROZZAPRETI.

strangozzi [strang-**goh**-tsee] thick Tuscan spaghetti.

strangujët [stran-goo-shuht] GNOCCHI with tomato sauce and plenty of basil, an AR-BËRESH dish.

straniero/a [strahn-**yair**-oh] foreign. Wine lists are often divided into *vini Italiani* ('Italian wines') and *vini stranieri* ('foreign wines').

strapazzate [strah-pat-**zah**-tay] scrambled (eggs).

strascinati [strah-shee-**nah**-tee] pasta similar to FETTUCCI-NE or TAGLIATELLE. Sometimes called *penchi*.

strattu [strah-**too**] in Sicily, tomato purée, lit. 'extract' (*estratto*) of tomato, made by cooking sundried tomatoes and straining the result.

stravecchio [strah-**veck**-yo] of a cheese, 'extra aged', in other words even older than a *vecchio*. *Stravecchio* cheeses are typically aged for three years. Cheeses aged for four years or more are sometimes described as *stravecchione*. Brandy can also be *stravecchio* (the equivalent of X.O. on the label).

Strega [stray-gah] a herbal DIGESTIVO coloured with saffron and flavoured with mint, consumed, in fiction, by Don Vito Corleone in Mario Puzo's *The Godfather*. The name means 'witch', an allusion to the ancient traditions of witchcraft supposed to have existed in its place of manufacture, Benevento (Campania).

streppe e caccialà [strep-ay ay catch-ah-**lah**] a simple shepherds' dish native to the Maritime Alps of Liguria. It consists of roughly-made piece of pasta boiled in water with cabbage leaves, turnips and potatoes.

striguli [**stree**-goo-lee] the young shoots of the bladder campion (*Silene vulgaris*), once common in cooking, now much rarer.

stringozzi [streen-**gots**-ee] thick spaghetti from Umbria,

very similar to PICI.

stroncatelli [stronka-**tell**-ee] spaghetti-like pasta made of flour and egg, popular in Italian Jewish cuisine and traditionally eaten at Rosh Hashanah (Jewish New Year).

strozzapreti [strots-ah-**pray**-tee] pasta shape, the 'priest strangler', so called because it resembles a rope or rolled length of cloth.

strucolo [**stroo**-ko-loh] a strudel.

struffoli [**stroo**-foh-lee] honey-glazed pyramids of fried dough (Campania).

strutto [**stroo**-toh] lard, reduced pork fat, used in baking and in stews. Not to be confused with the more sophisticated LARDO.

struzzo [**stroo**-tsoh] ostrich, reared in ever increasing numbers throughout Italy.

stufato, stufatino [stoo-**fah**-toh, stoo-fah-**tee**-noh] a stew; as an adjective, *stufato* means stewed, braised (fem. *stufata*).

stuzzichini [stoots-ee-**keen**-ee] titbits, finger food that can be served on toothpicks (*stuzzicadenti*).

su ordinazione [soo ore-dee-nats-ee-**own**-ay] made to order.

sucameli [soo-kah-**may**-lee] PASTA CORTA served with honey and cinnamon in Puglia and Sicily.

succo [**soo**-ko] juice (pl. *succhi*).

sugeli [**soo**-jay-lee] pasta characteristic of the Ligurian alps, small *gnocchetti* traditionally served with BRUZZO cheese.

sughitti [soo-**gee**-tee] sweetmeats made from cooked must and cornflour (Marche).

sugna [**soon**-ya] suet.

sugo [**soo**-goh] sauce or gravy.

suino [**swee**-noh] pig.

superiore see VINO.

Supertuscan term coined by the America wine critic Robert Parker to describe wines from the BOLGHERI region, and also TIGNANELLO from CHIANTI, which revolutionised Italian winemaking in the 1970s by their pioneering use of Bordeaux grape varieties (Cabernet Sauvignon, Cabernet Franc, and Merlot). Italian wine classification rules originally prevented these wines from obtaining DOC status. This situation has now been rectified.

suppa quatta [**soo**-pah **kwah**-tah] a thick soup from Sardinia made by pouring meat stock over alternate layers of bread, PECORINO, parsley and nutmeg and slowly baking until the bread has absorbed the stock and a crust has formed on top.

supplemento [soop-lay-**main**-toh] an extra charge or supplement.

supplì [soop-**lee**] Roman rice balls, stuffed with cheese.

sursuminata [soor-soo-mee-**nah**-tah] scrambled eggs with tomatoes (Calabria).

susamelli [soo-zah-**may**-lee] honey-sweetened sesame-seed biscuits.

susianella [soo-zee-ann-**eh**-lah] a well seasoned sausage of pork meat and offal, from the province of Viterbo, Lazio.

susina [soo-**zeen**-ah] plum (pl. *susine*).

tacchino [tack-**ee**-noh] turkey.

tacconelle = SAGNE A PEZZE.

tacconi [tack-**own**-ee] large squares (pasta shapes).

taccula [**tack**-oo-lah] *sa taccula* is a Sardinian way of cooking small birds, typically blackbirds, by cooking them in myrtle leaves.

taggiasche, olive [oh-**lee**-vay tadge-**ass**-kay] the *taggiasca* is a highly prized variety of black olive from Liguria, used for eating and to make oil.

tagliata [tal-**yah**-tah] lit. 'cut'; *tagliata di manzo* is grilled beef entrecôte seasoned with herbs and served in slices. The inside of the meat must be left rare.

tagliatelle [tal-ee-ah-**tell**-ay] broad ribbons of egg pasta.

tagliato/a a cubetti [tal-ee-ah-toh ah koo-**bet**-ee] diced.

taglierini [tal-ee-ay-**ree**-nee] thin noodles.

tagliolini [tal-yoh-**lee**-nee] egg-pasta noodles.

tajarelle [tie-ah-**rell**-ay] rib-bon pasta from Abruzzo.

tajarin [tie-ah-**reen**] egg noo-dles (Piedmont).

taleggio [tal-**edge**-oh] a mild cow's milk cheese from Lombardy, similar in texture to STRACCHINO. Taleggio now enjoys DOP status.

tanaceto [tan-ah-**chay**-toh] tansy, a bitter plant used to make the DIGESTIVO called *arquebuse*. Tansy is held to be good at soothing headaches and joint pain, and effective in preventing infestations of worms.

tannura [tan-**oo**-rah] a small clay oven (Sicily).

tarallo [tar-**al**-oh] a ring-shaped bread roll or biscuit, typical of southern Italy. The diminutive form is *taralluccio*; pl. *taralli*.

tarantella [tar-an-**tay**-lah] tuna SALAME from Taranto, Puglia.

tarocco [tar-**ock**-oh] blood orange.

tartina [tar-**teen**-ah] a canapé or open sandwich

tartufato/a [tar-too-**fah**-toh]

flavoured with truffles.

tartufo [tar-**toof**-oh] truffle, a rare, expensive and highly prized arboreal fungus, a significant component of Italian cuisine (*see box*).

Truffles

The truffle is a fungus that grows on or around the roots of trees. The relationship is mutually beneficial, the truffle gaining access to the tree's reserves of carbohydrate and sucrose, the tree benefitting from the water and minerals that the truffle absorbs from the soil. There are several types of truffle to be found in Italy, all of them either white or black.

The best known **white truffle** is the *Alba madonna*, the 'diamond of Piedmont', which grows in the Langhe area and in the countryside around Alba. Also found in Croatia, it flourishes around the roots of oak, hazel, poplar and beech trees and is harvested in autumn, coinciding with the town's annual truffle fair. Another kind of white truffle, the *Tuber magnatum pico*, grows in the Marche and other parts of central Italy.

There are two main kinds of **black truffle**: *Tuber aestivum*, the summer truffle, which grows throughout Italy; and *Tuber melanosporum*, which grows well with oak, hazel and hornbeam. The finest examples come from Norcia and Spoleto in Umbria. Acqualagna, a town in the Marche, is famous for its international festivals for white, black and summer truffles.

Fittingly, given their elusive nature, truffles are 'hunted' by farmers who use sniffer dogs specially trained for the purpose. In former times pigs were used, but they had a dangerous tendency to eat the truffles once they had found them, possibly as a result of becoming over-excited by the truffle's scent, which bears a resemblance to that of the porcine sex hormone. Dogs are more tractable. The preferred breed in Italy is the *Lagot-to romagnolo*, a gundog native to Romagna with an obedient nature and a gentle mouth. Such dogs are known as *cani da tartufo* [**kah**-nee dah tar-**too**-foh]: 'truffle hounds'. For a long time the best-known truffle hound in Italy was Diana, who belonged to the Italian-Croatian farmer Giancarlo Zigante. In 1999 she found, near Buje in Croatia, what was recorded in the *Guinness Book of Records* as the largest truffle in the world, weighing 1.31 kg (2lb 14oz). Though this truffle was found in Croatia it did much to stimulate the industry around Alba in Italy, largely as a result of Zigante's imaginative PR initiatives which included refusing to sell the truffle, getting it cast in bronze, giving a lavish banquet to celebrate its discovery, and having Diana hunt truffles on stage in Carnegie Hall. Diana's Croatian record remained unbroken for several years until the autumn of 2007, when a truffle hound named Rocco and his owner Luciano Savini discovered a gigantic example near Pisa, Tuscany. This weighed 1.5kg (3.3lb) and Savini determined to offer it to the highest bidder. At the end of a high-profile auction held simultaneously in Macau, Hong Kong and Florence, the flamboyant Macau casino owner Stanley Ho hazarded USD 330,000 for the truffle, making it at the time not only the largest but also the most expensive ever recorded.

tartufo di mare [tar-**too**-foh dee **mah**-ray] a Venus clam, the 'Warty Venus' as opposed to the smooth variety, which is known as *cappa liscia*.

Taurasi [ta-oo-**rah**-zee] perhaps the finest red wine from southern Italy. Made mainly from the AGLIANICO grape, grown in Campania.

tavola calda [**tah**-voh-lah

kal-dah] literally 'hot table', a restaurant or snack bar offering pre-cooked food.

tavolozza [tav-oh-**lots**-ah] literally, a painter's palette; by association an assortment, e.g. *tavolozza di formaggi morbidi*: an assortment of soft cheeses.

tazza [**tah**-tsa] cup

té [tay] tea.

tegame [tay-**gah**-may] a pan, hence *al tegame* or *al tegamino*, braised.

tellina [tay-**lee**-nah] wedge clam, a shellfish related to the COZZA and the VONGOLA (pl. *telline*).

temolo [**tay**-moh-loh] grayling (freshwater fish).

tendaio [ten-**die**-oh] a medium-flavoured cow's milk cheese made in Castiglione di Garfagnana, Tuscany.

tenerine [tay-nay-**ree**-nay] sweet cherries.

tenero/a [ten-**air**-oh] tender.

Teroldego [tay-**roll**-day-goh] grape from Trentino-Alto Adige producing fresh and fruity reds.

A *tellina*, a wedge shell.

testa di maiale [**taste**-ah dee my-**ah**-lay] pig's head.

testa in cassetta [**taste**-ah een cass-**ett**-ah] brawn or head cheese, a SALUME made from leftover pork cuts, especially meat taken from the head.

teteun [tay-tay-**oon**] a SALUME made from cooked cows' udders, salted and heavily seasoned with herbs, considered a delicacy in the Valle d'Aosta.

tiella [tee-**ell**-ah] a layered dish named after the utensil it is cooked in and thus occurring in many manifestations. In general it is a kind of hotpot, containing whatever is at hand: rice, potatoes, shellfish, vegetables and so on.

tigelle [tee-**jell**-ay] small circular pastries like Scotch pancakes, waffles or drop scones (Emilia-Romagna), eaten with a variety of sweet and savoury toppings or fillings.

tiglio, fiori di [**fyor**-ee dee tee-lyoh] lime blossom.

Tignanello [tee-nya-**nell**-oh] premier wine from the CHIANTI region, which blends native SANGIOVESE with Cabernet Sauvignon and Cabernet Franc. Because of the inclusion of non-native grape varieties, it was not permitted to call itself a Chianti according to the classification rules of the time (the early '70s), and the producer left the Chianti consortium amid much publicity. Tignanello became famous as one of the SUPERTUSCANS. Today the rules have changed, and should it wish, it may now label itself a Chianti.

timballo [teem-**bal**-oh] a baked dish of one staple ingredient (potatoes, pasta or rice) with accompaniments such as cheese, mushrooms, tomatoes.

timo [tee-moh] thyme.

timpano see TIMBALLO.

tinca [**teen**-ka] tench.

Tintilia [teen-**tee**-lee-ah] a red grape native to Molise, producing a strong regional wine of the same name.

tiramisù [tee-rah-mee-**soo**] a rich dessert of sponge cake layered with MASCARPONE, sharpened with brandy or other spirit together with ESPRESSO, and sprinkled with chocolate powder. The name means 'pick-me-up', an allusion to its supposed restorative properties.

tisana [tee-**zah**-nah] herb tea.

toast not a toasted slice of bread, but a ham and cheese sandwich, a *croque monsieur*.

Tocai Friulano [tock-**ay** free-ool-**ah**-noh] white grape used to produce the peachy wine of Friuli, not to be confused with the Tokaj wine of Hungary. In theory EU regulations forbid the Italian wine to use the name Tocai, but the rule is not strictly adhered to.

tocco di funghi [**tock**-oh di **foon**-gee] a 'touch of mushrooms', a Ligurian sauce comprising PORCINI cooked in wine with parsley, garlic, pine nuts and butter. Some versions also use tomatoes.

toma [**toh**-mah] a type of alpine cow's milk cheese made from skimmed milk, similar to the French *tomme de Savoie*. A good example is *Toma di Gressoney*, made in the Valle d'Aosta. *Tomini* are small cheeses from Piedmont preserved in oil and spices.

tonnarelli [ton-ah-**rell**-ee] egg pasta cut in fine strands, similar to spaghetti. They are very typical of Roman cuisine, often served with the sauce known as CACIO PEPE.

tonnato [tonn-**ah**-toh] served with a tuna mayonnaise or *salsa tonnata*. *Vitello tonnato*, cold poached veal served in a tuna mayonnaise, is an effective collision of tastes and a widely popular dish.

tonno [**tonn**-oh] tuna. *Tonno alla siciliana* [see-chee-lee-**ah**-nah] is tuna cooked with garlic, wine and mint or basil, served in a tomato sauce, to which olives and capers are sometimes added.

tonno del Chianti [ton-oh del kee-**ahn**-tee] not tuna at all, but pork, cooked long and slowly until it is meltingly tender. Cut up while still warm, it is mixed with olive oil and herbs. For best results, use meat from CINTA SENESE pigs, and serve with *cannellini al* FIASCO.

topinambur [toh-pee-**nam**-boor] Jerusalem artichoke.

topini [toh-**pee**-nee] Tuscan potato-filled RAVIOLI.

torcetti [tore-**chet**-ee] malted biscuit loops from Piedmont.

torchi [**tork**-yo] PASTA CORTA shaped like hand torches or flashlights.

torciglione see SERPENTONE.

torcinello [tor-chee-**nell**-oh] a lamb's intestine filled with sweetbreads, well seasoned and grilled (pl. *torcinelli*).

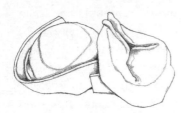

Tortellini, a type of *pasta ripiena* said to resemble the navel of Venus.

torcolo [**tor**-koh-loh] a large, thick CIAMBELLA.

tordi [**tor**-dee] thrushes. See UCCELLINI.

tornagusto [tor-nah-**goo**-stoh] literally a 'taste reviver', a sauce devised by Vincenzo Corrado, chef at the court of Naples in the 18th century, to reawaken the jaded palates of his employers. His *tornagusto* for PROSCIUTTO *di Parma* was made of a mixture of sugar and lard: Corrado died at the age of 103; he may not have eaten too much of his own cooking.

torresano [tor-ay-**zahn**-ee] farmed pigeon or squab (pl. *torresani*).

Torrette [toh-**reh**-tay] DOC red wine from Valle d'Aosta.

torrone [tor-**oh**-nay] nougat, either hard or soft.

torta [**tore**-tah] 1. a cake, tart, flan or pie; 2. chickpea flat-bread from Livorno, Tuscany.

torta al testo SEE CRESCIA.

torta salata [**tore**-tah sa-**lah**-ta] the 'savoury pie' of Liguria, filled with whatever ingredients are to hand.

tortelli [tor-**tell**-ee] PASTA RIPI-ENA similar to RAVIOLI. *Tortelli di zucca*, stuffed with pump-kin, are popular in northern Italy; *tortelli di patata* are Tuscan potato-filled ravioli.

tortellini [tor-tell-**een**-ee] small egg pasta pockets origi-nally from Emilia-Romagna, made with a variety of fill-ings including ham, cheese, spinach and potato. *Tortellini* resemble the navel and there are a number of appealing stories about their origin. One relates that when Venus, Mars and Bacchus stopped one night at an inn near Bologna, the innkeeper could not resist peeping through the keyhole. Upon beholding Venus's exquisite navel, he rushed straight to the kitchen and recreated it in pasta form.

tortelloni [tor-tell-**own**-ee] large TORTELLINI.

tortiglioni [tor-tee-lee-**own**-ee] short, fat pasta tubes with grooves.

tortino [tor-**teen**-oh] a patty, e.g. *tortino di pesce*: fishcake.

tortora [**tor**-tor-ah] turtle dove.

Toscana see TUSCANY.

toscanelli [toss-kah-**nell**-ee] a white Tuscan FAGIOLI.

totano [toh-**tah**-noh] a type of squid, the end of its body shaped like an arrow (*see picture on p. 155*; pl. *totani*).

tovagliolo [to-vah-**lyoh**-loh] table napkin (*see box below*).

The art of folding table linen

If you have ever sat in a restaurant and marvelled at the work of art that is your serviette, you would appreciate the *magnum opus* of Matthias Geiger (d. 1630), a Bavarian professor at the University of Padua, whose *Tre Trattati* are three treatises on tablecraft. The first deals with the art of decorative table linen sculpture and is a step-by-step manual beginning with simple three-way geometric designs and progressing to more intricate confections including bishop's mitres, hunting dogs, lettuces, ships in full sail, wood grouse, the double-headed Habsburg eagle and lion of St Mark. The other two treatises deal with how to lay a table, the proper season for all viands, and how to trim, dress, carve and serve them.

---

tozzo [**tot**-so] a crumb or fragment.

tramezzini [tra-mets-**ee**-nee] sandwiches; a filling placed between two slices of square white bread, which is then cut into to triangles. Although very similar to the English prototype, they claim to have been in invented in Turin, and there is even a precise date: 1925. The name was dreamed up by the patriotic poet, aviator and First World War hero Gabriele d'Annunzio: in Mussolini's day there was a Fascist drive to rid the Italian language of what were seen as foreign barbarisms, thus 'sandwich' was deemed unacceptable. See also MARINETTI.

trancio [**tran**-choh] a slice (pl. *tranci*), e.g. *due tranci di pizza*.

tranquillo [tran-**kweel**-oh] still (not sparkling).

trattoria [trat-or-**ee**-ah] a restaurant, often family-run, and with an informal atmosphere.

Trebbiano [treb-**yah**-noh] white-wine grape grown throughout Italy and used to produce pale, dry wines such as FRASCATI.

treccia [**tray**-chah] a plait or braid, used of cheese such as MOZZARELLA or bread.

trenne [**trenn**-ay] hollow pasta tubes characteristic of Liguria, flattened on one side; *trennette* are a smaller equivalent.

Trentino-Alto Adige [tren-**tee**-noh ahl-toh **ah**-dee-jeh] northeastern region of Italy bordering Austria and Switzerland. It has a dual gastronomic heritage, Trentino being distinctly Italian and Alto Adige being Tyrolean. Game stews and alpine cheeses are the hallmark of the latter, while POLENTA, freshwater fish from the lakes and pasta characterise the former. Many of the grape varieties have German names: Rosenmuscateller, Gewürztraminer— an appropriately *gemütlich* reminder of Austria.

tretarielle see MENUZZE.

tria see CICERI.

tricolore [tree-koh-**lore**-ay] lit. 'three colours', a style of many republican flags. The Italian tricolor dates back to the Repubblica Cispadana, a northern Italian state set up by Napoleon in 1796 (the stripes on its flag were horizontal; the vertically-striped flag seen today, with the same colours turned clockwise through 90°, was first used by patriots in the Risorgimento, the movement for Italian unity, and was adopted as the flag of the new Kingdom of Italy in 1861. In 1946 it was again officially adopted as the flag of the republic). In gastronomic terms the colours are also symbolic: green for forests and alpine pastures, or any number of indigenous strains of spinach, cabbage, wild herbs or artichokes; white for cheese and pasta; red for wine, CHIANINA beef, marbled sections of PROSCIUTTO, and glossy sun-ripe tomatoes.

tridarini [tree-dah-**ree**-nee] a type of PASTA GRATTATA.

triddi [**tridh**-ee] Puglian PASTA GRATTATA.

triglia [**tree**-lee-ah] red mullet. There are two kinds of mullet: *triglia di fango*, the 'mullet of the mud', thrives in shallow, sandy or muddy water; *triglia di scoglio* [**sko**-lee-oh], the 'mullet of the rocks' or striped red mullet, which lives in clearer, deeper water and has a better diet, is more highly prized.

tripoline [tree-poh-**lee**-nay] a wavy noodle named in honour of Italy's conquest of Tripoli.

trippa [**tree**-pah] tripe, once street food in most Italian cities, but now building up a gourmet following as CUCINA POVERA becomes more fashionable.

triscule [**trees**-koo-lay] wild strawberries (Friuli dialect).

trito/a [**tree**-toh] minced.

troccoli [**trock**-oh-lee] a coarse kind of TAGLIOLINI.

trofie, trofiette [**troh**-fee-ay, troff-**yet**-ay] PASTA CORTA in the form of flattened corkscrews.

trota [**troh**-tah] trout; there are many types, both freshwater and saltwater. *Trota salmonata* [sal-moan-**ah**-tah] is not a subspecies, it refers to a trout whose flesh is pink due to plenty of carotein in its diet.

trucioli [troo-**cho**-lee] 'wood shavings' a form of PASTA GRATTATA.

truffles see TARTUFO.

tuorlo d'uovo [**twor**-low **dwoh**-voh] egg yolk (pl. *tuorli*).

turcinuna [tour-chee-**noon**-ah] lamb or goat intestines stewed with onions and lemon, Sicily.

turtiddi [tour-**tidh**-ee] sweet fried GNOCCHI (Calabria).

Tuscany region of central Italy known as much for its food and wine as for the cultural treasures of Florence and Siena. Tuscan land is good for agriculture, for vines and olives, and the woods are full of game. The cuisine is firmly tied to the land, and preparation is simple, the main ingredients, such as bread, meat and oil, being allowed to speak for themselves without the augmentation of elaborate sauces. Wild boar and steak are popular dishes, and the peppery beef stew known as PEPOSO is a classic. Tuscany produces some of the most famous of all Italian wines, including CHIANTI, BRUNELLO di Montalcino, Vino Nobile di Montepulciano, and the sweet dessert wine VINSANTO. There are fine Tuscan SALUMI, and truffles also abound.

tutto mare [**toot**-oh **mah**-ray] lit. 'all sea'; a seafood sauce.

uccelli scappati [oo-**chay**-lee ska-**pah**-tee] 'escaped' birds, morsels of liver, meat or sausage cooked in ways more usually associated with small birds and game, especially with POLENTA, when the traditional song birds or migratory birds are not available.

uccellini [oo-chay-**lee**-nee] small game birds such as *tordi* (thrushes), *merli* (blackbirds) or *allodole* (larks). Shooting is very popular in Italy, but it is becoming a contentious subject as bird numbers dwindle and conservationists become more vocal.

uccelletto [oo-chay-**leh**-toh] general term for a small game bird, although there is a Tuscan bean dish, *fagioli all'uccelleto*, in which the beans are slow-cooked in a tomato and sage sauce of a type normally served with game birds.

Umbria a beautiful region known for the Apennine mountain ranges and their foothills, for the enchantments of Lake Trasimene, and for the great monastery of St Francis at Assisi, with its cycle of frescoes by Giotto. The hillside city of Perugia is the capital and there are numerous picturesque smaller towns. The cuisine of Umbria is varied and reflects a quietly prosperous pastoral heritage dating back to Etruscan times. Wild pigeon, roast suckling pig, black truffle omelette and chilli-infused sauces are characteristic of the region. NORCIA sausages are famous. SAGRANTINO di Montefalco is a well-regarded wine.

umbrichelli [oom-bree-**kell**-ee] pasta noodles typical of Orvieto in Umbria.

umido, in [oo-mee-doh] stewed, in other words cooked slowly in liquid, in a covered pan.

uova di bufala [**wove**-ah dee **boo**-fah-lah] 'buffalo's eggs', small MOZZARELLA cheeses.

uovo [**wove**-oh] egg (pl. *uova*); *uova fritte* = fried eggs; *uova strapazzate* = scrambled eggs.

uova e curcuci see OVA.

uva [oo-vah] grapes; *uva bianca/nera* = white /red grapes; *uva passa* [**pah**-sah], *uva secca* [**say**-kah] and *uvetta* [oo-**vay**-tah] are raisins.

uva spina [oo-vah **spee**-nah] gooseberry.

Valle d'Aosta small, north-western region renowned for dramatic alpine views, feudal castles and abundant wildlife. The Parco del Gran Paradiso was Italy's first national park. The regional cuisine shows notable examples of French and Swiss influence, and because of the cold climate, the emphasis is on preserved food: cheese and cured meats. Polenta is the local staple. Lardo d'Arnad, made from the fat of chestnut-fed pigs, is famous. *Caffè Valdostano*, served in a communal cup with many spouts, is flavoured with orange and laced with grappa. See grolla dell'amicizia.

Val di Chiana see Chianina.

Valdobbiadene [val-dob-**yah**-day-nay] wine-growing area of Treviso province in the Veneto, known for its prosecco.

valeriana [val-ay-ray-**ahn**-ah] valerian; *valernianella* is lamb's lettuce.

Valpolicella [val-pol-ee-**chell**-ah] popular red wine made in the province of Verona, the lighter varieties often being served chilled somewhat in the manner of young Côtes du Rhône. The fine wines of Valpolicella are Amarone and Recioto. See also Ripasso.

vaniglia [van-**eel**-ya] vanilla.

vapore [vah-**pore**-ay] steam; *al vapore* = steamed.

varolo, variolo [vah-**roh**-loh, vah-ree-**oh**-loh] Venetian dialect for sea bass.

Varzi [**vart**-see] a village in the Oltrepò Pavese area of Lombardy, famous for its salame.

vastedda [vah-**stedh**-ah] typical Sicilian street food. A sandwich, filled with cheese and/or cold meats.

VdT *vino da tavola*, table wine.

vecchio/a [**veck**-yo] old; of a cheese, aged.

vegetariano/a [vay-jay-tar-ee-**ahn**-oh] vegetarian.

velenoso/a [vay-lay-**noh**-zoh] poisonous.

venature [vain-at-**oor**-ray] veining; in a ham, streaks.

vendemmia [vain-**dem**-ya] grape harvest; *vendemmia tardiva* [tar-**dee**-vah] is late harvest.

Venerdì gnoccolar [vain-air-**dee** nyock-**oh**-lar] 'Gnocchi Friday' in Verona, the first Friday after Shrove Tuesday, a festival devoted to gnocchi. The master of ceremonies is the Papà del Gnocco, whose sceptre is a giant fork impaling a *gnocco*.

Veneziana [vain-ay-tzee-**ahn**-ah] 1. pertaining to Venice; 2. *veneziane* are almond-glazed brioches.

ventresca [vain-**tray**-skah] the tender underbelly of tuna (though the word can be applied to other fish) often served as grilled steaks.

ventricina [vain-tree-**chee**-nah] a pork SALUME from the Abruzzo.

verde all'italiana, salsa [**vair**-day al-ee-tal-**yah**-nah] Italian green sauce of olive oil, garlic, parsley, anchovies, capers, cucumbers and vinegar.

Verdicchio [vair-**dee**-kee-oh] grape from the Marche producing white wines, generally crisp and pleasant. Verdicchio dei Castelli di Jesi is highly respected.

verdure [vair-**doo**-ray] vegetables; *verdure di stagione* [stadge-**own**-ay] are seasonal vegetables.

Verduzzo [vair-**doot**-soh] grape from the Friuli region, yielding fruity, perfumed white wines.

Vermentino [vair-main-**tee**-noh] white-wine grape cultivated in Sardinia and in coastal regions of Tuscany and Liguria. Produces dry wines that go well with fish.

vermicelli [vair-mee-**chay**-lee] literally, 'little worms', very thin pasta used in soups.

vermouth (in Italian, *vermut*) a dry fortified wine, flavoured with herbs, said to have been invented in Turin in the late 18th century. Italian vermouth comes in two varieties, dry white and sweet red (made sweet with the addition of caramel). White vermouth is often used in cooking as a substitute for white wine. The best known brands of Italian vermouth are MARTINI and CINZANO.

Vernaccia [vair-**natch**-ah] 1. a white-wine grape grown in central Italy, used in Tuscany, for the DOC Vernaccia di San Gimignano; 2. Vernaccia di Serrapetrona is a ruby-red dessert wine from the Marche.

verza [**vairt**-sah] Savoy cabbage, usually boiled, sautéed or stuffed.

verze ripiene [**vairt**-say ree-pee-**ay**-nay] stuffed Savoy cabbage leaves.

vialone [vee-a-**lone**-ay] a type of rice used for RISOTTO.

vicentina, alla [vee-chen-**tee**-nah] 'Vicenza style'. BAC-CALÀ *alla vicentina* is stockfish cooked with onions and milk.

vincisgrassi [veen-chees-**grah**-see] LASAGNE from the Marche made with the addition of béchamel sauce. Vincisgrassi is a corruption of the name of Alfred Candidus Ferdinand, Prince of Windisch-Grätz, commander of the Austrian forces against Napoleon at the siege of Ancona (1799). The dish was allegedly created for him by a local chef and constitutes an interesting fusion, encountered elsewhere in northern Italian cooking, of lean local produce and middle-European creaminess.

vinicolo [vee-**nee**-koh-low] wine-producing; *produzione vinicola* = wine production.

vino [**vee**-noh] wine. Italy is one of Europe's most important producers of wine, and the range is vast. Major grape varieties and types of wine are indexed by name (e.g. BAROLO, SANGIOVESE) throughout this book.

Basic wine terms

Colour: *rosso* (red); *bianco* (white); *rosato* (rosé).

Taste: *secco* (dry; *abboccato* (semi-dry); *amabile* (semi-sweet); *dolce* (sweet); *frizzante* (sparkling).

Quality: *vino del paese* (country wine); *vino da tavola* (table wine); *vino della casa* (house wine); *vino sfuso* (loose wine, which you can order by the carafe, *caraffa*). *Vino superiore* indicates a grade above the standard wine; more prestigious still is the *Riserva*. *Vino d'annata* is vintage wine.

Wine classification

In Italy, as in other wine-producing nations, the quality of a wine depends on measurable factors such as grape type, climate, soil and age. Immeasurables, such as the resourcefulness, integrity and vision of individual wine producers, are the subject of as much debate in Italy as they are elsewhere. Italy also has stringent wine laws that dictate what grapes may be used for what wines, and for blended wines, in what proportions those grape varieties may be mixed.

Wine (and also some foods, such as olive oil, balsamic vinegar and parmesan cheese) are carefully classified in Italy. Wine is bottled and sold under four classifications which commonly appear on wine bottle labels, either written out in full or in abbreviated form: VdT, IGT, DOC and DOCG.

VdT: *vino da tavola*, for the most part good, honest table wine that varies from area to area and vintage to vintage.

IGT (*Indicazione geografica tipica*): used to classify wines that are produced to a high standard in a defined geographical area but which do not meet the stricter requirements necessary for a DOC or DOCG classification.

DOC (*Denominazione di origine controllata*): used to classify wine that is produced to strict standards in specified regions. In its zeal to implement the new system in the wake of new legislation in 1992, the awarding bodies handed out what many felt to be an excessive number of DOCs, with the result that it was soon necessary to implement a new. 'super' classification:

DOCG (*Denominazione di Origine Controllata e Garantita*). Here the product's quality and authenticity is 'guaranteed' by official, government-licensed tasters.

Reading a wine label

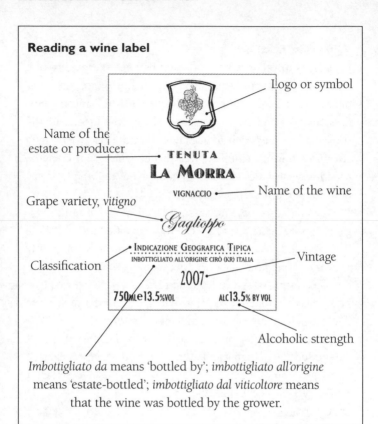

Logo or symbol

Name of the estate or producer

TENUTA
LA MORRA

VIGNACCIO — Name of the wine

Grape variety, *vitigno*

Gaglioppo

INDICAZIONE GEOGRAFICA TIPICA
INBOTTIGLIATO ALL'ORIGINE CIRÒ (KR) ITALIA

Classification

Vintage

2007

750ᴍʟ℮13.5%ᴠᴏʟ   ᴀʟᴄ13.5% ʙʏ ᴠᴏʟ

Alcoholic strength

Imbottigliato da means 'bottled by'; *imbottigliato all'origine* means 'estate-bottled'; *imbottigliato dal viticoltore* means that the wine was bottled by the grower.

vino speziato [vee-noh spets-ee-**ah**-toh] spiced, mulled wine, served in winter.

vino da tavola [**vee**-noh da **tah**-voh-la] table wine.

vino visciolato [**vee**-no vee-sholl-**ah**-toh] red wine infused with wild cherries.

Vinsanto [veen-**san**-toh] or Vin Santo; amber-coloured dessert wine from Tuscany, typically made from TREB-BIANO or MALVASIA grapes, which are traditionally dried on straw to concentrate the sugars. The name means 'holy

wine'; it has been suggested that *Vinsanto* was once used as Communion wine. Another theory is that it was first made on the Ionian island of Zakynthos (Zante in Italian). The wines vary in sweetness; some are almost dry.

violino di capra [vee-oh-lee-noh dee **kah**-prah] 'The goat's fiddle', a goat leg marinated in wine with juniper berries, bay leaves and other seasoning. Originally from the Valtellina and Valchiavenna in Lombardy it is carved in a striking manner, the joint held like a violin, the carving knife its bow. Tradition says that once started, the whole thing must be eaten before the guests may leave the table.

virtù [veer-**too**] spring vegetable soup.

visciole [**vee**-show-lay] bitter cherries.

viscotta [vee-**scot**-ah] Sicilian dialect, a biscuit.

vite [**ee**-tay] vine (pl. *viti*).

vitello [vee-**tell**-oh] calf, veal.

vitigno [vee-**teen**-yo] grape variety.

vongole [**von**-go-lay] clams (sing. *vongola*). *Spaghetti alle vongole*, a popular dish in the Veneto, is served with a sauce of garlic, parsley, pepper and olive oil with a hint of dried chilli.

vongole veraci [**von**-go-lay vay-**rah**-chee] carpet shell clams, distinguishable from

Two types of *vongole*. The simple *vongola* (above) has a pale brown or greyish shell patterned with a distinctive zigzag. *Vongole veraci* (shown below) have darker shells marked with radiating vertical bands.

vongole by the bands on their shells (*see illustration on previous page*).

vredocchie [vray-**dock**-ee-ay] indented GNOCCHI from Molise, traditionally served with cauliflower in the dish *vruocchele con vredocchie*.

vuliata [voo-lee-**ah**-tah] in Puglia, a bread roll baked with olives (*puccia e uliate*).

weinsuppe [**vine**-zoo-peh] *zuppa di vino* in Italian, a light soup made with white wine, beef broth, egg yolks and cream seasoned with cinnamon, characteristic of Trentino-Alto Adige. *Terlanerweinsuppe*, made in the town of Terlano, is the best known version.

wine see VINO.

xeres [**tsay**-rez] sherry.

zabaglione [tsah-buy-**own**-ay] a creamy dessert made with beaten eggs, sugar and MARSALA.

zafferano [tsa-fay-**rah**-noh] saffron, the stamen of a particular kind of crocus (*Crocus sativus*), cultivated mainly in the Marche, Abruzzo and Sardinia. It is a highly prized (and highly priced) flavouring ingredient for soups, cakes and pasta. It was introduced into Italy from Spain in the 13th century, by a Dominican monk, from Navelli in the Abruzzo, who first came across the plant in Toledo, while attending a meeting on the extirpation of heresy. The saffron crocus throve in Italian soil and made fortunes for the residents of Navelli and also the town of L'Aquila, which celebrated its wealth by building and endowing churches, libraries and colleges.

zammù [tsah-**moo**] a Sicilian drink flavoured with anise.

zampa, zampetta [**tsam**-pah, tsam-**peh**-tah] foot or claw.

zampone [tsam-**poh**-nay] a SALUME from Modena. Seasoned pork stuffed into the skin of a pig's front leg. It is typically served in slices, often accompanied by lentils, beans, pickles, etc.

zanchetta [tsan-**ket**-ah] small fish, particularly the scaldfish; small fry.

zappatora, alla [tsap-ah-**tore**-ah] 'navvy style'; see CARRE-TIERA.

zelten [tsel-ten] a rich cake of dried fruit and nuts, from Trentino-Alto Adige.

zenzero [tsen-tsay-roh] ginger.

zeppola [tsepp-oh-lah] a fritter, in southern Italy; *zeppole di San Giuseppe* are fritters for Saint Joseph's Day, made in Naples, noted for their rich, creamy fillings.

zeraria [tsay-**rah**-ree-ah] a pork SALUME from Liguria.

zibba [tsee-bah] also known as *merca*, a Sardinian name for glasswort or SALICORNIA. In *muggine sulla zibba*, a grey mullet is served on a bed of it.

Zibibbo [tsee-**bee**-boh] 1. a versatile grape from Sicily, the basis both of simple table wines and distinctively flavoured GRAPPAS; 2. sweet wine made from the grape.

zighe [tsee-gay] see ARSELLE.

zighera [tsee-**gay**-rah] round curd cheese, seasoned or smoked, from Trentino.

zigoinr [tsee-**goin**-er] a species of wild oregano unique to the area surrounding Cortina d'Ampezzo in the Veneto Dolomites, used to flavour PUCCIA DI CORTINA.

zigrinate [tsee-gree-**nah**-tay] small snails.

zimino, in [tsee-**mee**-noh] used mainly of fish, meaning cooked in a sauce of finely minced onion and celery with spinach or chard. Some versions also include tomatoes.

zippuli [tsee-poo-lee] a Sardinian term for fritters. See ZEPPOLA.

zite, ziti [tsee-tay, tsee-tee] large, tubular MACCHERONI originally from Southern Italy, also known as *boccolotti*, *zitoni*, *zituane* or *candele*.

zolfini [tsoll-**fee**-nee] a Tuscan variety of FAGIOLI, known also as *fagioli burrini* ('butter beans'), suitable for cooking *al* FIASCO. Tradition relates that before retiring to bed, Tuscan labourers would fill their empty terracotta wine flasks with beans and leave them nestling overnight in the dying embers of the hearth. The following day the slowly-cooked beans would form the basis of a sustaining snack.

zolletta [tsoll-**et**-ah] a cube, e.g. *zollette di zucchero*, sugar-lumps.

zucca [**tsoo**-kah] pumpkin, squash, marrow (pl. *zucche*).

zucchero [**tsoo**-keh-roh] sugar. *Zucchero greggio* [**gredge**-oh] = brown sugar.

zucchine, zucchini [tsoo-**keen**-ay, tsoo-**keen**-ee] courgettes, zucchini; baby marrows.

zuccotto [tsoo-**kot**-oh] a dome-shaped SEMIFREDDO with a sponge exterior and an ice cream and candied fruit filling.

zuf [tsoof] in Friuli, a gruel or porridge made of corn POLENTA and milk. It can also refer to a dish of creamed pumpkin.

zufi [tsoo-fee] a fermented RICOTTA from northern Piedmont.

zuncà see GIUNCATA.

zuppa [tsoo-pah] soup.

zuppa inglese [tsoop-ah een-**glay**-zay] literally 'English soup,' the Italian version of trifle: layers of custard and chocolate cream, laced with ALCHERMES and containing crumbled sponge cake for texture. A plausible theory as to its origin is that the Dukes of Este instructed their chefs to recreate the dramatically rich English puddings they had been served at the court of Elizabeth I.

zuppa alla Pavese [tsoop-ah alla pah-**vay**-zay] see PAVESE.

zuppetta [tsoop-**et**-ah] 1; a little soup; 2: a cream and sponge slice from Naples.

USEFUL PHRASES

Cordiality, courtesy, a polite use of the conditional tense, a clearly expressed readiness to part with money and sincerely expressed gratitude all go a long way in Italy. The following twelve basic phrases are well worth rehearsing until you have them by heart. They can be attached with minimal adaptation to virtually any word, phrase or concept contained in this book.

I. THE TWELVE BASICS

Good morning *Buon giorno* [bwon **jor**-noh]
Good afternoon *Buon pomeriggio* [bwon pom-air-**ee**-joh]
Good evening *Buona sera* [bwon-nah-**say**-rah]
Please *Per favore* [pair fah-**voh**-ray]
Thank you *Grazie* [**graht**-see-ay]
I would like *(Io) vorrei* [**ee**-oh voh-**ray**-ee]
We would like *Vorremmo* [voh-**rem**-oh]
He would like *(Lui) vorrebbe* [**loo**-ee voh-**reb**-ay]
She would like *(Lei) vorrebbe* [**lay**-ee voh-**reb**-ay]
The bill please *Il conto per favore* [eel **kon**-to pair fah-**voh**-ray]
This is for you *Ecco a lei!* [**eck**-oh ah **lay**-ee] (when giving a tip)
Goodbye and thank you *Arrivederci, grazie!* [ah-reev-ay-**dair**-chee **grat**-see-ay!].

II. FINDING A RESTAURANT

The next step is to find a good restaurant. Research on the internet sometimes works, and guide books can be a great help. But nothing can beat asking real people for their opinion. Concierges, chambermaids, policemen, the couple at the next table at breakfast—all these are fair game and may well be able to impart useful local knowledge.

Where is the nearest restaurant?
Dove si trova il ristorante più vicino? [**Doh**-vay see **troh**-va eel ree-stor-**an**-tay **pyoo** vee-**chee**-noh]

Is there a restaurant near here?
C'è un ristorante qui vicino? [Chay oon ree-stor-**an**-tay kwee vee-**chee**-noh]

Can you recommend...
   ...a good restaurant?
   ...an exclusive restaurant?
   ...a reasonably priced restaurant?
   ...a restaurant where they serve authentic Italian cooking?
Mi può consigliare... [Mee **pwo** con-see-lee-**ahr**-ay]
   ...un buon ristorante? [oon **bwon** ree-stor-**an**-tay]
   ...un ristorante esclusivo? [oon ree-stor-**an**-tay es-kloo-**zee**-voh]
   ...un ristorante a prezzi ragionevoli? [oon ree-stor-**an**-tay a **pret**-see radge-on-**ay**-vole-ee]
   ...un ristorante dove si servono autentica cucina italiana? [oon ree-stor-**an**-tay **doh**-vay see **sair**-voh-no ow-**ten**-tee-ka koo-**cheen**-ah ee-tal-ee-**ahn**-ah?]

Where is the best pizzeria?
Dov'è la migliore pizzeria? [**doh**-veh la meel-**yaw**-ray peets-ay-**ree**-ah?]

Can you recommend a bar where they sell good snacks?

Mi può consigliare un bar dove vendono spuntini buoni? [Mee **pwo** con-see-lee-**ahr**-ay oon bar doh-vay **vain**-doh-noh spoon-**teen**-ee **bwon**-ee?]

We would like a quiet candlelit dinner.
Vorremmo una tranquilla cena a lume di candela. [voh-**ray**-moh oon-ah tran-**kweel**-ah **chay**-nah a **loo**-may dee kan-**day**-lah]

We would like to go to a place with dancing and live music.
Vorremmo andare in un luogo con dansing e un gruppo live. [voh-**rem**-oh ann-**dar**-ay een oon **lwoh**-goh kon **dan**-seeng ay oon **groo**-poh lyve].

III. BOOKING

The likelihood is that you will either ask a concierge to make a booking for you or, failing that, take your chances and explore the city, town or village. If you feel sufficiently confident to make a booking yourself, the following phrases will be useful.

I'd like to make a reservation.
Vorrei fare una prenotazione. [Voh-**ray**-ee **fah**-ray oo-na pray-no-tats-**yoh**-nay]

What time do you open this evening?
A che ora apre stasera? [a kay **ore**-ah **ah**-pray stah-**say**-rah?]

I would like to book a table for seven o'clock / 7.30.
Vorrei prenotare un tavolo per le sette / le sette e mezzo. [voh-**ray**-ee pray-noh-**tah**-ray oon **tah**-voh-loh pair lay **say**-tay / **say**-tay ay **med**-zo]

There are four of us.
Siamo quattro. [see-**ah**-moh **kwat**-roh]

1, 2, 3, 4, 5, 6, 7, 8, 9, 10, 11, 12
uno, due, tre, quattro, cinque, sei, sette, otto, nove, dieci, undici, dodici
[**oo**no, **doo**ay, tray, **cheen**kway, say, **set**-ay, **ot**-oh, **noh**-vay, dee-**ay**-chee, **oon**-dee-chee, **doh**-dee-chee]

IV. BASIC QUESTIONS

Is there a fixed price menu?
C'è un menù a prezzo fisso? [chay oon may-**noo** a **prets**-oh **fee**-soh]

Can we bring the children?
Possiamo portare i bambini? [poh-see-**ahm**-oh por-**tah**-ray ee bam-**bee**-nee]

Is there a high chair?
C'è un seggiolone? [chay oon sedge-oh-**loan**-ay]

Do you have vegetarian dishes?
Hanno piatti vegetariani? [**ah**-noh pee-**att**-ee vay-jay-tah-ree-**ahn**-ee]

I am allergic to...
  ...nuts.
  ...dairy products.
  ...gluten.
Sono allergico / allergica... [**soh**-no ah-**lair**-jee-koh / ah-**lair**-jee kah]
  ...ai noci [ah-ee **noh**-chee]
  ...ai latticini [ah-ee lah-tee-**chee**-nee]
  ...al glutine [ahl **gloo**-tee-nay]

Can you prepare dishes without...?
Possono preparare piatti senza...? [**poh**-so-noh pray-pah-**rah**-ray pee-**att**-ee **sent**-sah...]

Do you take credit cards?
Accettano carte di credito? [ah-chay-**tah**-noh kar-tay dee **kray**-dee-toh]

V. ARRIVING AT THE RESTAURANT

If you have not booked and the restaurant seems busy, ask if you can wait. The manager will tell you if a table will be available soon or apologise is he is unable to accommodate you (*mi dispiace, ma siamo al completo stasera*: I'm sorry but we're fully booked this evening). Once a table is available, or if you have already booked, you will need to choose where to sit.

I have a reservation in the name of ––––––––.
Ho una prenotazione a nome di –––––––– [**oh** oo-na pray-no-tats-**yoh**-nay ah **noh**-may dee]

Can we wait for a table?
Possiamo aspettare un tavolo? [poh-see-**ah**-moh ass-pet-**ah**-ray oon **tah**-voh-loh]

Can we come back in half an hour?
Possiamo tornare tra media ora? [poh-see-**ah**-moh tor-**ah**-ray tra **may**-dee-ah **ore**-ah]

May we sit here?
Possiamo sedermi qui? [poh-see-**ah**-moh say-**dair**-mee kwee]

Can we sit...
  ...inside / outside?
  ...by the window?
  ...in the corner?
Possiamo sedermi... [Poh-see-**ah**-moh say-**dair**-mee]
  ...all'interno / all'esterno? [ahl een-**tair**-noh / ahl es-**tair**-noh]
  ...vicino alla finestra? [vee-**chee**-noh alla fee-**nay**-stra]
  ...all'angolo? [ahl **ahng**-goh-loh]

We are in a hurry.
Siamo in fretta. [See-**ah**-moh een **fret**-ah]

VI. ORDERING YOUR MEAL

You are seated and ready to order drinks and inspect the menu. Try to gauge the relative seniority of the staff and to judge if it would be better to use the more respectful *Signora* or *Signore* when attempting to attract their attention. Get a fix on where the bathrooms are, especially if you are with children. Remember that children are welcomed even if they make a lot of noise.

Decoding an italian menu

A typical menu will list courses as follows: ***antipasti*** (*appetisers*); ***primi piatti*** (pasta and risotto); ***secondi piatti*** with ***contorni*** (meat and fish dishes with accompanying vegetables), followed by ***formaggi*** (cheese) and ***dolci*** (desserts). You do not have to order all courses. It is perfectly acceptable just to have a starter and a pasta dish, or a starter, meat and dessert. Fixed-prize menus are also sometimes available, for example a ***menu del giorno*** at lunchtime or a ***menu degustazione*** (taster menu).

Waiter! Waitress!
Cameriere! Cameriera! [kam-ay-ree-**ay**-ray! kam-ay-ree-**ay**-rah!]

Madam! Sir! Miss!
Signora! Signore! Signorina! [seen-**yore**-ah! seen-**yore**-ay! seen-yore-**ee**-nah!]

We would like something to drink.
Vorremmo qualcosa da bere. [vor-**em**-oh kwal-**koh**-sah da **bay**-ray]

Could we have the menu please?
Potremmo avere il menu? [pot-**rem**-oh ah-**vay**-ray eel may-**noo**]

Do you have a menu in English?
Avete un menu in inglese? [av-**ay**-tay oon may-**noo** in een-**glay**-zay]

May I see the wine list?
Potrei vedere la carta dei vini? [pot-**ray**-ee vay-**day**-ray la **kar**-ta day-ee **vee**-nee?]

We would like a bottle of...
  ...still water.
  ...sparkling water.
  ...this wine.
Vorremmo una bottiglia di... [voh-**rem**-oh oo-na bot-**eel**-ya dee]
  ...acqua liscia [**ack**-wah-**lee**-shah]
  ...acqua frizzante. [**ack**-wah freets-**ann**-tay]
  ...questo vino. [**kway**-stoh **vee**-noh]

I would like...
The little girl would like...

The little boy would like...
Vorrei... [voh-**ray**-ee]
La bambina vorrebbe... [la bam-**bee**-nah voh-**reb**-ay]
Il bambino vorrebbe... [eel bam-**bee**-noh voh-**reb**-ay]

For me / her / him/ us / them.
Per me / lei / lui / noi / loro [pair may / **lay**-ee / **loo**-ee / noy / **lore**-oh]

What are the dishes of the day?
Quali sono i piatti del giorno? [**kwah**-lee **soh**-noh ee pee-**aht**-ee del **jore**-noh?]

What do you recommend?
Che cosa mi consiglia? [kay **koh**-sah mee kon-**seel**-ya?]

We are not ready to order.
Non siamo pronti per ordinare. [no see-**am**-oh **pron**-tee pair ore-dee-**nah**-ray]

We would like what they're having.
Vorremmo un piatto uguale al loro. [voh-**rem**-oh oon pee-**att**-oh oo-**gwal**-ay al **lore**-oh]

We'd like to order now.
Vorremmo ordinare ora. [voh-**rem**-oh ore-dee-**nah**-ray **oar**-ah]

I'd like something light.
Vorrei qualcosa di leggero. [voh-**ray**-ee kwal-**koh**-za dee lay-**jay**-roh].

Which wine do you recommend for the fish / meat / dessert?
Quale vino mi consiglia per il pesce / la carne / il dolce? [kwah-lay **vee**-

noh mee kon-**see**-lee-ah per il **pay**-shay / **kar**-nay / **doll**-chay]

We would like to share a selection of antipasti.
Vorremmo condividere una selezione di antipasti. [voh-**rem**-oh kon-dee-**vee**-day-ray oo-na say-lets-ee-**own**-ee dee an-tee-**pas**-tee]

Which vegetables are in season?
Quali sono le verdure di stagione? [**kwah**-lee **soh**-no lay vair-**doo**-ray dee stadge-**own**-ay]

May I have...
  ...spinach with the steak?
  ...**more bread, oil and vinegar?**
  ...**some ice?**
Posso avere... [**poss**-oh ah-**vay**-ray]
  ...*gli spinaci con la bistecca?* [Lee spee-**natch**-ee kon la bis-**teck**-ah]
  ...*più pane, olio e aceto balsamico?* [pee-oo **pah**-nay, **oh**-lee-oh ay atch-**ay**-toh bal-**sammy**-coe]
  ...*un po' di ghiaccio* [oon **poh** dee **gyah**-choh]

I'd like to try...
  ...a local cheese.
  ...a traditional dish.
Vorrei provare... [voh-**ray**-ee proh-**vah**-ray]
  ...*un formaggio locale.* [oon for-**madge**-oh low-**kah**-lay]
  ...*un piatto tradizionale.* [oon pee-**att**-toh tra-dee-tsee-oh-**nah**-lay]

Please bring...
  ...another bottle of wine / water.
  ...another orange juice.
  ...a knife / spoon / napkin.

...a fork.
...the salt and pepper.
Si prega di portare... [see **pray**-gah dee por-**tah**-ray]

   ...*un'altra bottiglia di vino / d'acqua.* [oon **al**-tra boh-**teel**-ya dee
      vee-noh / **d'ack**-wah]

   ...*un altro succo d'arancia* [oon **al**-tro **soo**-koh dah-**ran**-cha]

   ...*un coltello / cucchiaio / tovagliolo* [kol-**tell**-oh / cookie-**eye**-oh /
      to-vah-**lyoh**-loh]

   ...*una forchetta* [**oo**-na fore-**kett**-ah]

   ...*il sale e il pepe.* [eel **sah**-lay ay eel **pay**-pay]

What grape variety is this wine?
Che vitigno è questo vino? [kay vee-**teen**-yo eh **kway**-stoh **vee**-noh]

Just a drop [when the waiter offers to pour you more wine]
Solo un goccio. [**soh**-loh oon **gotch**-oh]

VII. SPECIAL NEEDS & REQUESTS

NB: For dietary requirements, see IV. Basic Questions.

Could you heat this [baby] bottle for me?
Potrebbe fare scaldare questo biberon? [poh-**treb**-ay **fah**-ray scal-**dah**-
ray **kway**-stoh bee-bay-**ron**]

Where is the bathroom?
Dov'è il bagno? [doh-**vay** eel **ban**-yo?]

Please could you close the window/door.
Potrebbe chiudere la finestra / porta. [poh-**treb**-ay kee-**oo**-day-ray la
fee-**nays**-trah / **pore**-tah?]

Please could you open the window/door.
Potrebbe aprire la finestra / porta. [poh-**treb**-ay ap-**ree**-ray la fee-**nays**-trah / **pore**-tah?]

Is this spicy?
È questo piccante? [ay **kway**-stoh pee-**kahn**-tay?]

Does this contain.....?
Questo contiene.....? [**kway**-stoh kon-tee-**ain**-ay]

Is this sweet?
È questo dolce? [ay **kway**-stoh **doll**-chay?]

VIII. WHEN THINGS GO WRONG

I did not order...
  ...this dish.
  ...this drink.
  ...this wine.
Non ho ordinato... [non oh ore-dee-**nah**-to]
  ...questo piatto. [**kway**-stoh pee-**att**-oh]
  ...questa bevanda. [**kway**-stah-bay-**van**-dah]
  ...questo vino. [**kway**-stoh **vee**-noh]

I ordered...
  ...the vongole / the lamb / the tiramisu.
  ...orange juice / sparkling water.
Ho chiesto... [oh kee-**ay**-stoh]
  ...le vongole / l'agnello / il tiramisù. [lay **von**-go-lay / lan-**yell**-oh / eel tee-ram-ee-**soo**]
  ...succo d'arancia / acqua frizzante [**soo**-koh dah-**ran**-cha / **ack-**

wah free-**tsahn**-tay]

We have been waiting a long time.
Abbiamo atteso per lungo tempo. [ab-**yah**-moh at-**ay**-zoh pair **loon**-go **tame**-poh]

This food / coffee is cold.
Questo cibo / caffè è freddo. [**kway**-stoh **chee**-boh / kah-**fay** ay **fred**-oh]

This is underdone.
Questo è poco cotto/a. [**kway**-stoh ay **poh**-ko **kot**-oh/ah]

This is overcooked.
Questo è troppo cotto/a. [**kway**-stoh ay trop-oh **kot**-oh/ah]

Excuse me, but the wine is corked.
Scusi, ma il vino sa di tappo. [**skoo**-zee ma eel **vee**-noh sa dee **tah**-po]

IX. PAYING THE BILL

Could I have the bill please?
Il conto per favore. [eel **kon**-toh pair fah-**voh**-ray]

May I pay with a credit card?
Posso pagare con una carta di credito? [**poss**-oh pah-**gah**-ray kon oona **kar**-tah dee **kray**-dee-toh]

Is service included?
Il servizio è incluso? [eel sair-**veets**-ee-oh ay een-**kloo**-zoh]

The bill isn't right.
Il conto non torna. [eel **kon**-toh non **tare**-nah]

Keep the change.
Tenga il resto. [teng-ah eel **ray**-stoh]

We will pay all together
Pagheremo tutti insieme [pah-gay-**ray**-moh **toot**-een-see-**ay**-may]

We will all pay separately
Facciamo alla romana (in the 'Roman' way, the equivalent of going Dutch) [fatch-**yam**-oh alla roh-**man**-ah]

We've eaten really well here
Abbiamo mangiato molto bene. [ab-ee-**am**-oh man-**jah**-toh **mole**-toh **bay**-nay]

The food was great.
Il cibo era ottimo. [eel **chee**-boh air-ah **ott**-eem-oh]

Could you call me a taxi?
Potrebbe chiamarmi un taxi. [poh-**treb**-ay kya-**mar**-mee oon **tak**-si]

X. IN THE BAR, CAFÉ OR GELATERIA

It is important to remember, when ordering in cafés or bars, that you should pay at the cash desk (*cassa*) and then take your receipt (*scontrino*) to the bar or to collect your order. The essential thing to be aware of in bars is the difference between bar service and table service. Do not order at the bar and then surreptitiously attempt to sit at a table.

I'd like a small / medium / large ice cream please.
Vorrei un gelato piccolo / medio / grande per favore. [voh-**ray** oon jay-**lah**-toh **pee**-koh-loh / **may**-dee-oh / **gran**-day pair fah-**voh**-ray]

I'd like one scoop / two scoops....
   ...in a cone / in a cup...
   ..with a little whipped cream.
Vorrei una pallina / due palline... [voh-**ray**-ee **oon**-a pah-**lee**-nah / **doo**-ay pah-**lee**-nay]
   ...in un cono / in una coppetta... [een oon **koh**-noh / een oo-nah koh-**pet**-ah]
   ...con un po' di panna. [kon oon **poh** dee **pah**-nah]

I would like...
   ...a glass of———.
   ...two croissants.
   ...two jam tarts.
   ...one of those.
   ...a slice of that cake.
   ...two slices of pizza.
Vorrei... [voh-**ray**-ee]
   ...un bicchiere di--------. [ooh bee-kee-**ay**-ray dee]
   ...due cornetti. [**doo**-ay kor-**neh**-tee]
   ...due crostate di marmellata. [**doo**-ay kroh-**stah**-tay dee mar-may-**lah**-ta]
   ...uno di questi / una di queste. [**oo**-no dee **kway**-stee / **oo**-nah dee **kway**-stay]
   ...una fetta di questa torta. [oo-nah **fet**-ah dee **kway**-stah **tore**-tah]
   ...due fette di pizza. [doo-ay **fet**-ay dee **peet**-zah]

SLOVAKIA

VIENNA

BRATISLAVA

GERMANY

MUNICH

AUGSBURG

AUSTRIA

BUDAPEST

Basel

ZURICH

Salzburg

Innsbruck

HUNGARY

Bern

SWITZERLAND

TRENTINO
ALTO
ADIGE

Trento

FRIULI
VENEZIA
GIULIA

Udine

LJUBLJANA

ZAGREB

l. Maggiore

l. Como

l. Garda

Bergamo

VENETO

SLOVENIA

Trieste

CROATIA

VALLE
D'AOSTA

LOMBARDY

Vicenza

VERONA

Padua

VENICE

Istria

Rijeka

MILAN

Po

Mantua

TURIN

Asti

PIEDMONT

Alba

Parma

Reggio

EMILIA

ROMAGNA

Ferrara

BOSNIA &
HERZEGOVINA

Barolo

LIGURIA

Modena

BOLOGNA

Ravenna

SARAJEVO

GENOA

Rimini

Split

Lucca

Barolo

MONACO

Pisa

Livorno

Arno

FLORENCE

CHIANTI

Siena

SAN MARINO

Ancona

MARCHE

Adriatic

Ligurian
Sea

Bolgheri

TUSCANY

Perugia

Assisi

Sea

Elba

L. Trasimeno

UMBRIA

Tiber

Dubrovnik

Corsica

L'Aquila

Chieti

ABRUZZO

ROME

LAZIO

MOLISE

Foggia

BARI

CAMPANIA

PUGLIA

NAPLES

Avellino

Matera

Ischia

Capri

BASILICATA

Taranto

Tyrrhenian

Sea

Sassari

SARDINIA

CALABRIA

Cirò

Cagliari

Stromboli

PALERMO

MESSINA

Reggio
di Calabria

Ionian

Sea

SICILY

CATANIA

Syracuse

MEDITERRANEAN

ANNABA

TUNIS

ALGERIA

SEA

TUNISIA

MALTA

0   100 km
0   50 miles

N